A gift for:

From:

If you love this giftbook...

...you can find

other HELEN EXLEY® books like it on

www.helenexley.com

Helen Exley and her team have specialised in finding wonderful quotations for gifts of happiness, wisdom, calm and between families, friends and loved ones... A major part of Helen's work is to bring love and communication within families by finding and publishing the things people everywhere would like to say to the people they love.

Her books obviously strike a chord because they now appear in forty-five languages, and are distributed in more than eighty countries.

You can follow us on 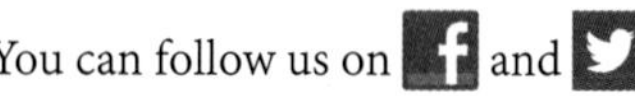

We all have the extraordinary
coded within us,
waiting to be released.

JEAN HOUSTON

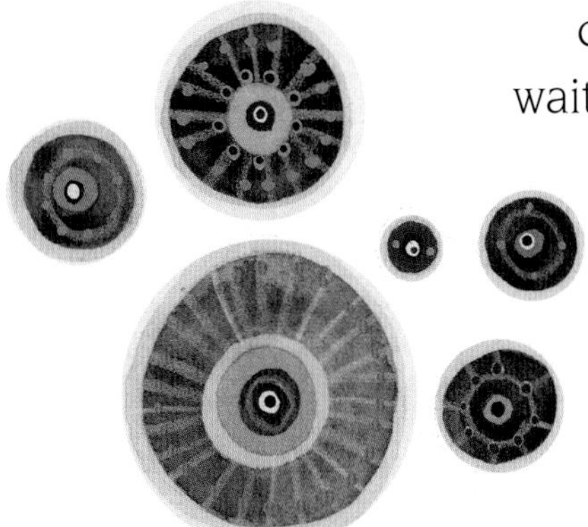

ILLUSTRATED BY JULIETTE CLARKE

EDITED BY DALTON EXLEY

Published in 2015, 2022 by Helen Exley® LONDON in Great Britain.

ISBN 978-1-78485-343-3 12 11 10 9 8 7 6 5 4 3 2 1

A copy of the CIP data is available from the British Library on request.
 Printed in China.

Helen Exley® LONDON, 16 Chalk Hill, Watford, Herts WD19 4BG, UK

www.helenexley.com

There are only two ways
to live your life.
One is as though nothing is a miracle.
The other is as though
everything is a miracle.

ALBERT EINSTEIN 1879 – 1955

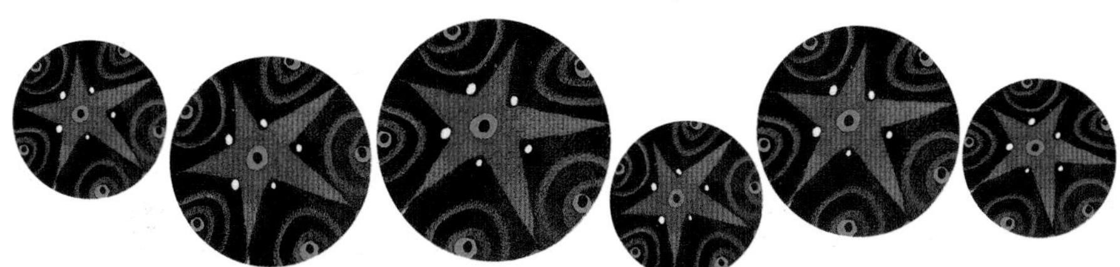

Let love and passion be behind everything, let it guide everything you do. Then just watch what happens – it's wonderful!

DR. DALTON EXLEY

There's always, always a way.

DAME KELLY HOLMES, B. 1970

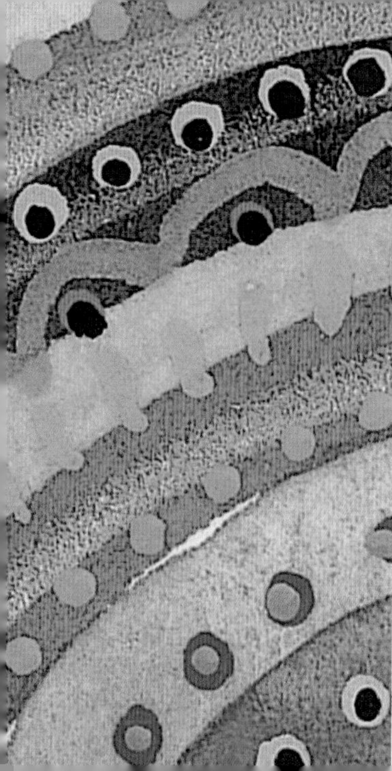

DECEMBER 30

If I am not concerned for myself,
who will be for me? But if I am only
concerned for myself,
what good am I? And if now is not
the time to act, when will it be?

HILLEL, C. A.D. 50

You can do anything if you have enthusiasm.

HENRY FORD 1863 – 1947

DECEMBER 29

You absolutely must believe in yourself – you've got to believe that you can do it. You can't let fear and negativity run your life.

PHYLLIS DILLER 1917 – 2012

The secret of success
is to really believe that you can achieve
and you will.

BILL CULLEN, B. 1942

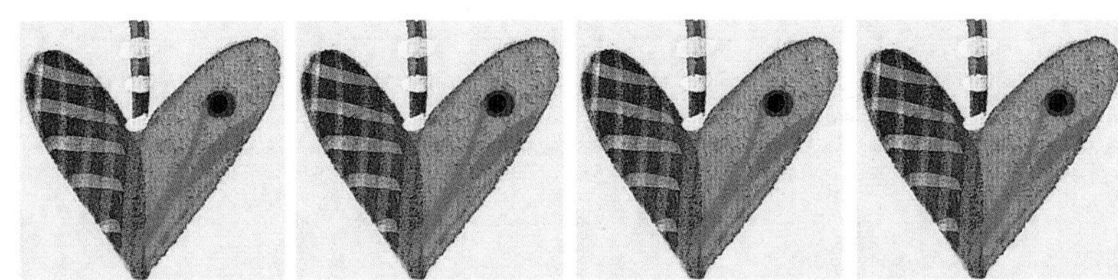

DECEMBER 28

Great things are done by people who think great thoughts and then go out into the world to make their dreams come true.

ERNEST HOLMES 1887 – 1960

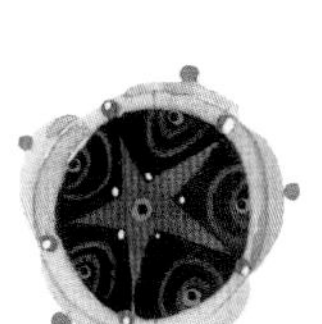
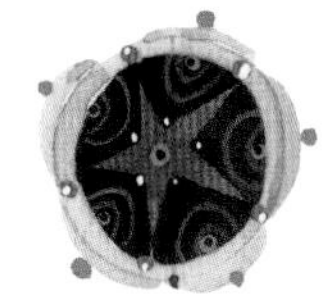
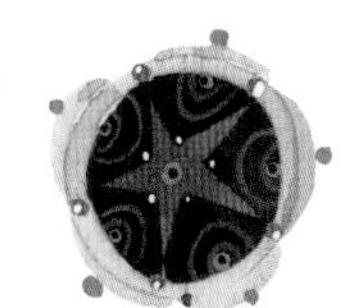
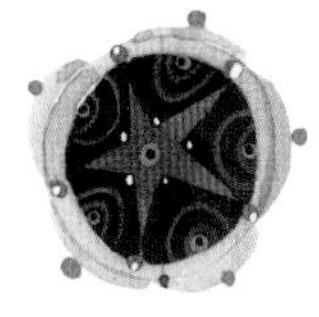
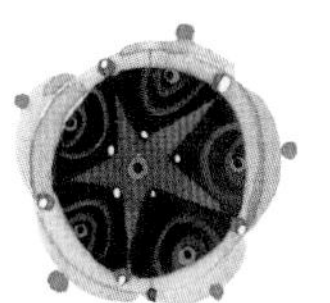

It always seems impossible until it's done.

NELSON ROLIHLAHLA MANDELA 1918-2013

DECEMBER 27

If we attend continually and promptly to the little that we can do, we shall ere long be surprised to find how little remains that we cannot do.

SAMUEL BUTLER 1835 – 1902

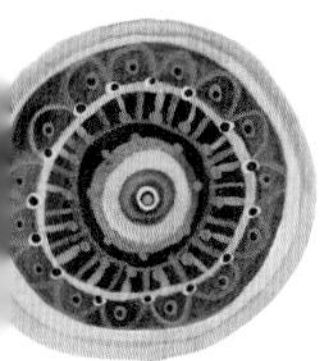
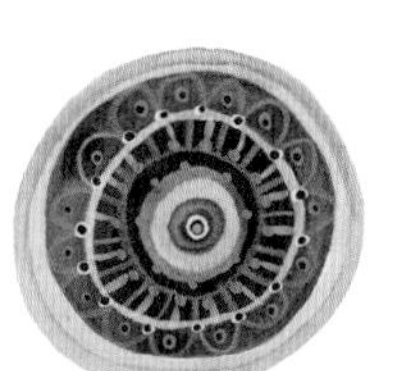
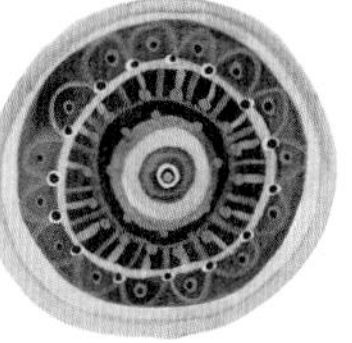
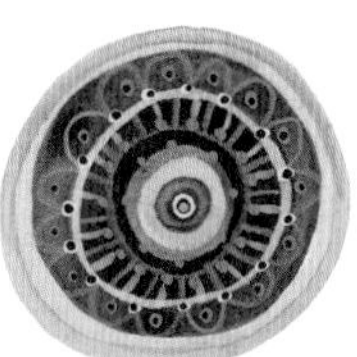
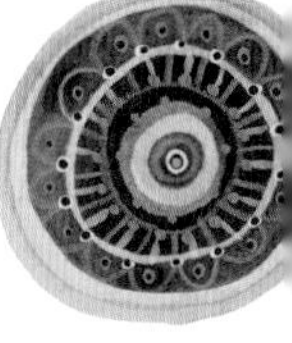

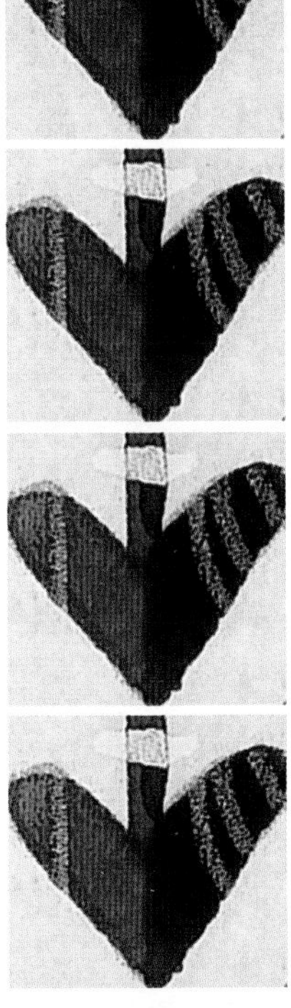

As long as you can start,
you are all right.
The juice will come.

ERNEST HEMINGWAY 1898 – 1961

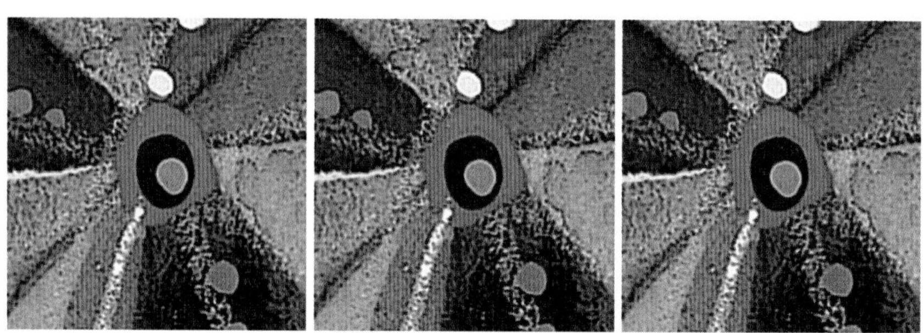

Life itself is the proper binge.

JULIA CHILD 1912 – 2004

The thing is always, always,
always make a start.
However small, just start.
You can build from there.

DR. DALTON EXLEY

Nothing great was ever achieved without enthusiasm. The way of life is wonderful; it is by abandonment.

RALPH WALDO EMERSON 1803 – 1882

JANUARY 9

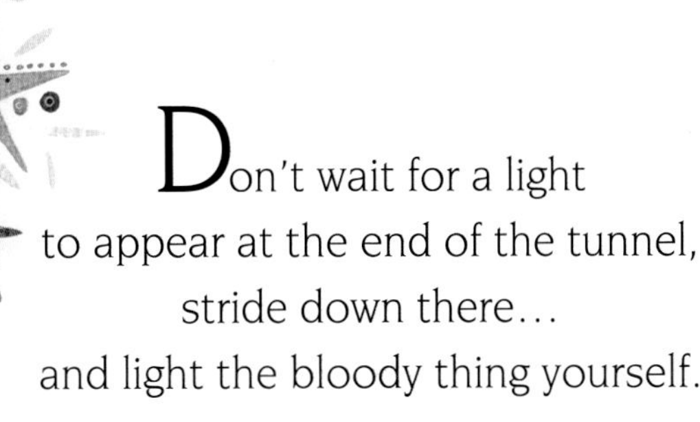

Don't wait for a light
to appear at the end of the tunnel,
stride down there…
and light the bloody thing yourself.

SARA HENDERSON, B. 1936

Whatever you attempt,
go at it with spirit. Put some in!

DAVID STARR JORDAN 1851 – 1931

I always believed that if you set out to be successful, then you already were.

KATHERINE DUNHAM 1909 – 2006

If you feel you were born with a special talent and have a destiny that's waiting to be uncovered, don't waste your life – discover it, develop it, become it! You will find your true self in the process and nothing will give you so much inner peace and ultimately contentment, than this.

DR. DALTON EXLEY

Take a chance!
All life is a chance.
The one who goes furthest
is generally the one
who is willing
to do and dare.

DALE CARNEGIE 1888 – 1955

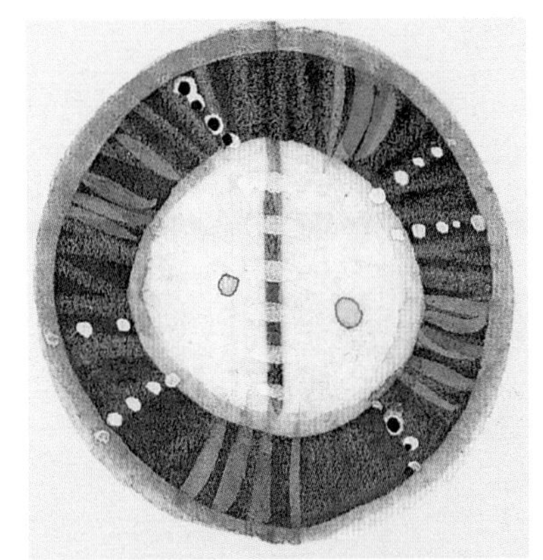

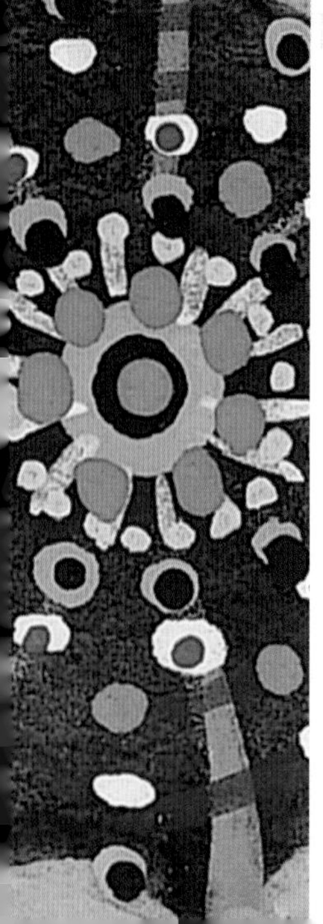

DECEMBER 22

ALL PEOPLE OF ACTION ARE DREAMERS.

JAMES E. HUNEKER

A pessimist sees the difficulty
in every opportunity
but an optimist does better -
he sees the opportunity in every difficulty.

SIR WINSTON CHURCHILL 1874 – 1965

DECEMBER 21

Always dream and shoot higher than you can do. Don't bother just to be better than your contemporaries or predecessors. Try to be better than yourself.

WILLIAM FAULKNER

You're the only one who can make the difference. Whatever your dream is, go for it.

EARVIN "MAGIC" JOHNSON, B. 1959

If you come to a thing with
no preconceived notions
of what that thing is, the whole world
can be your canvas.

WHOOPI GOLDBERG, B. 1955

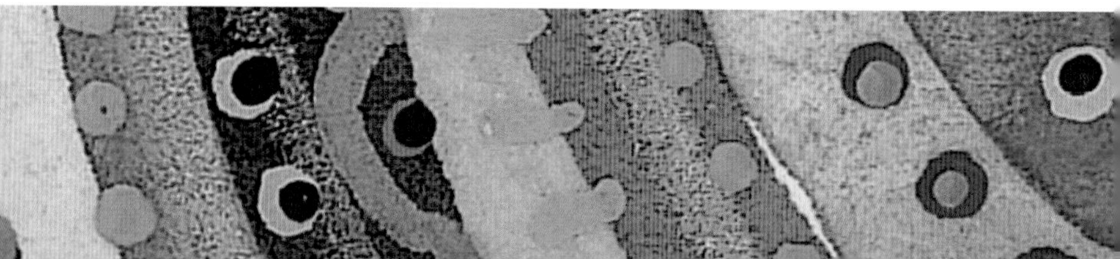

Be more positive.
Change your life for the better.
Instead of working out the reasons why you can't,
work out how you can.

DR. DALTON EXLEY

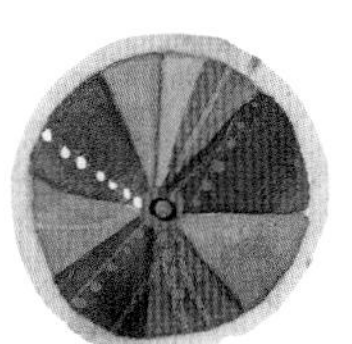
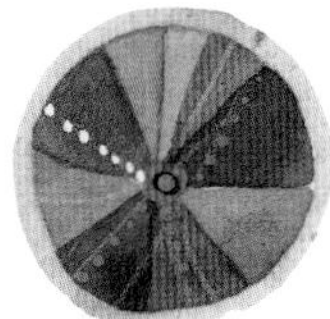
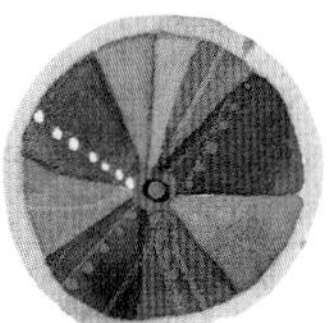
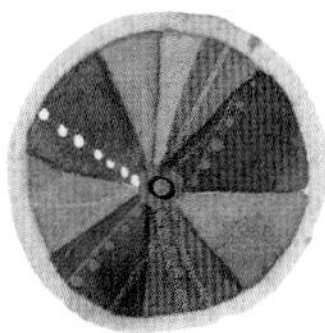

A PROBLEM IS THE PERFECT CHANCE FOR YOU TO DO YOUR BEST.

DUKE ELLINGTON 1899 – 1974

We should act more, think less,
and stop watching ourselves live.

NICOLAS DE CHAMFORT 1741 – 1794

We cannot do everything at once, but we can do something at once.

CALVIN COOLIDGE 1872 – 1933

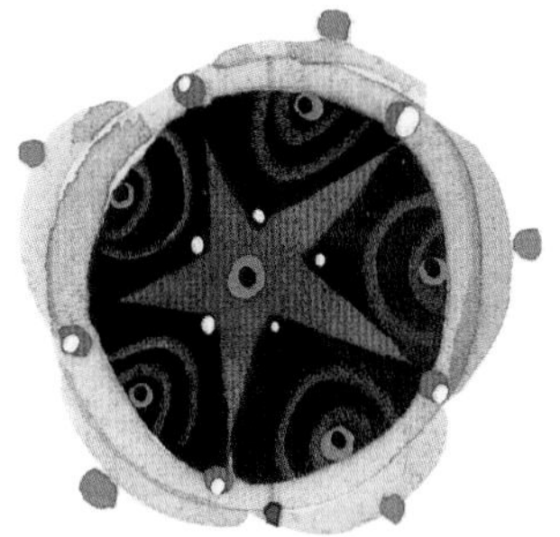

Make no little plans; they have no magic…
Make big plans, aim high in hope and work.

DANIEL H. BURNHAM

Progress results only from...
some men and women who refuse
to believe that what they know
to be right cannot be done.

RUSSELL W. DAVENPORT

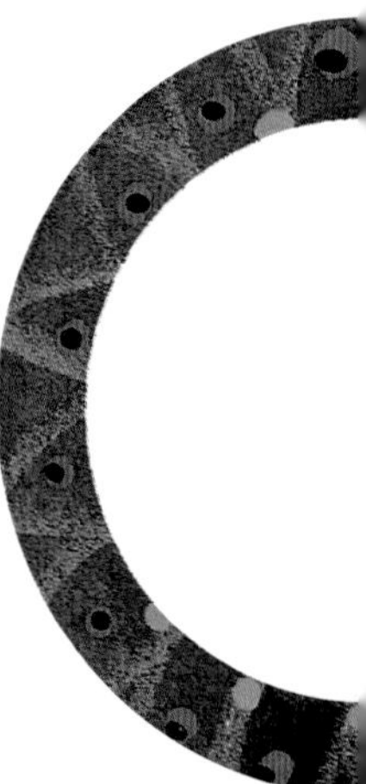

Just don't give up trying
to do what you really want to do.
Where there's love and inspiration,
I don't think you can go wrong.

ELLA FITZGERALD 1917 – 1996

We're given second chances every day of our life, we don't usually take them, but they're there for the taking.

ANDREW M. GREELEY, B. 1928

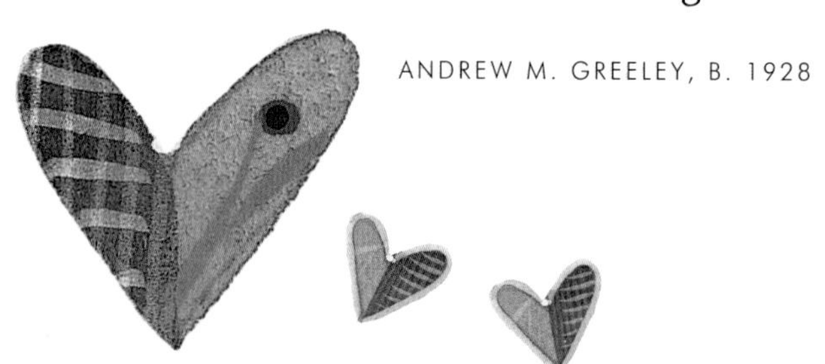

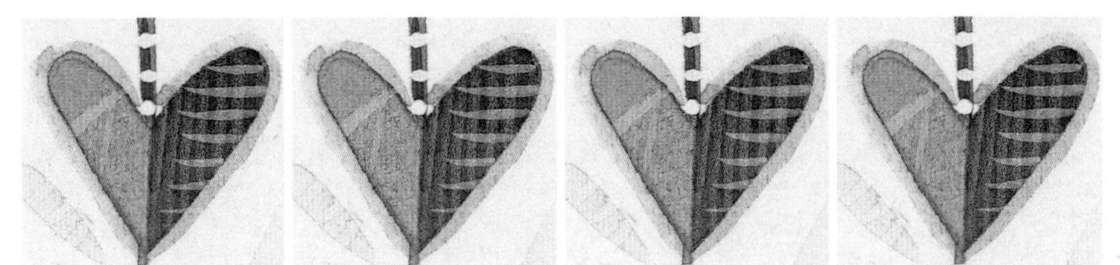

Clear your mind of "can't."

DR. SAMUEL JOHNSON 1709 – 1784

DECEMBER 15

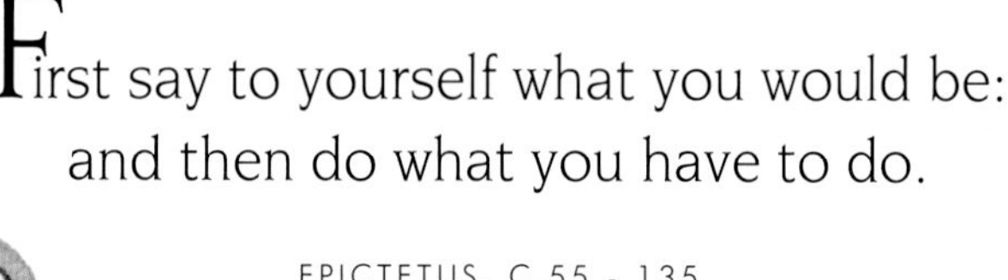

First say to yourself what you would be: and then do what you have to do.

EPICTETUS, C.55 - 135

Know your strengths and play to them.

JAMES CAAN

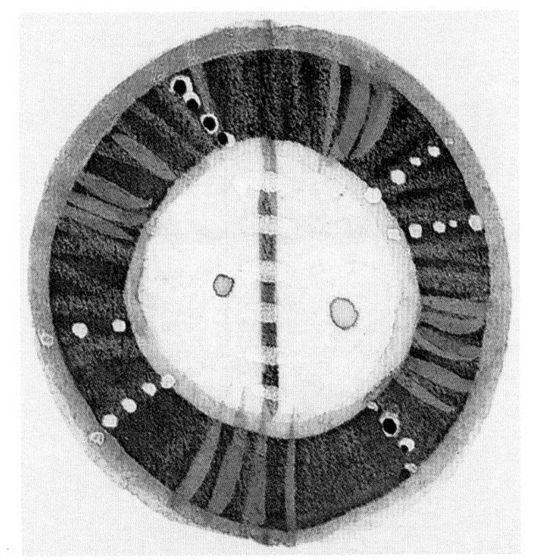

The great successful people of the world
have used their imagination...
they think ahead and create their mental
picture, and then go to work, materializing
that picture in all its details, filling in here,
adding a little there, altering this a bit
and that a bit, but steadily building
– steadily building.

ROBERT COLLIER 1885 – 1950

Success, failure, up, down, winner or loser.
A waste of time or time well spent. Most of this is in your mind.
A state of mind. You can just decide to be more positive,
to choose peace and happiness over stress and unhappiness,
to love, to live. This is real success. Everything else is a bonus.

DR. DALTON EXLEY

Follow your passion,
and success will follow you.

ARTHUR BUDDHOLD

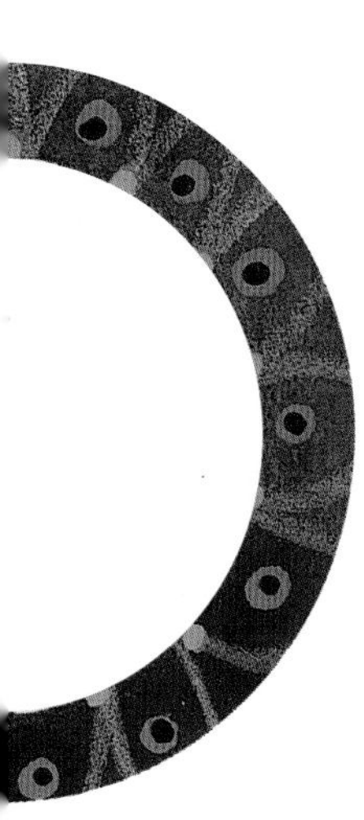

There is nothing you can't do
if you put your mind to it
and believe in yourself.
You just have to listen
to your own drummer
and not somebody else's.

DEREK BEEVOR, B. 1955

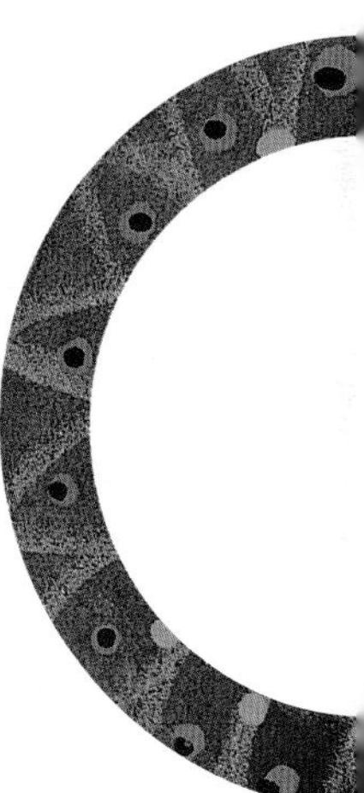

Set your goals high and aim for the stars, but be humble enough to accept – graciously – that it's fine and desirable to fall short.

ANNA FREUD

WHEN YOU CEASE TO DREAM
YOU CEASE TO LIVE

MALCOLM S. FORBES 1919 - 1990

It's only by giving it your all,
risking everything you have that you can possibly
find out how far you can really go.

DR. DALTON EXLEY

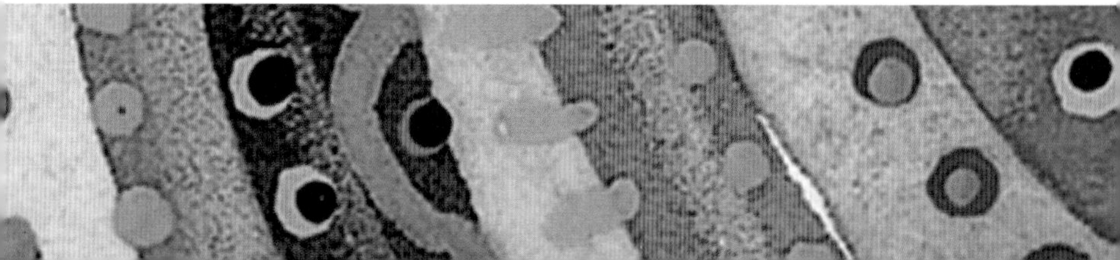

Attempt the impossible
in order to improve
your work.

BETTE DAVIS 1908 – 1989

Every ceiling, when reached, becomes a floor, upon which one walks as a matter of course and prescriptive right.

ALDOUS HUXLEY 1894 – 1963

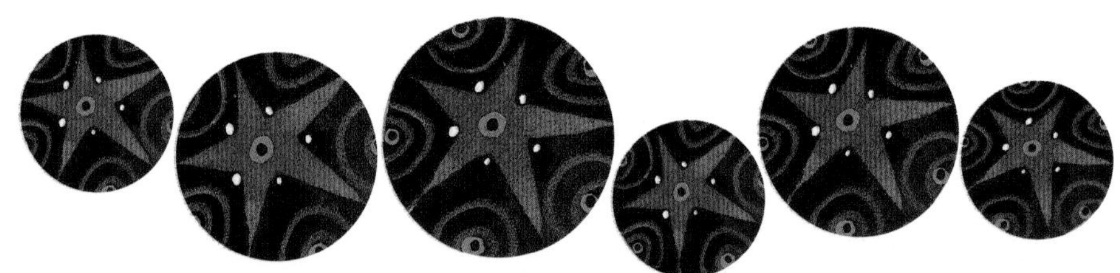

Positive actions today
will make your tomorrow the future
that you are dreaming about.

BILL CULLEN, B. 1942

When we nurture and inspire the human spirit, we say yes to the world.

HOWARD BEHAR, B. 1944

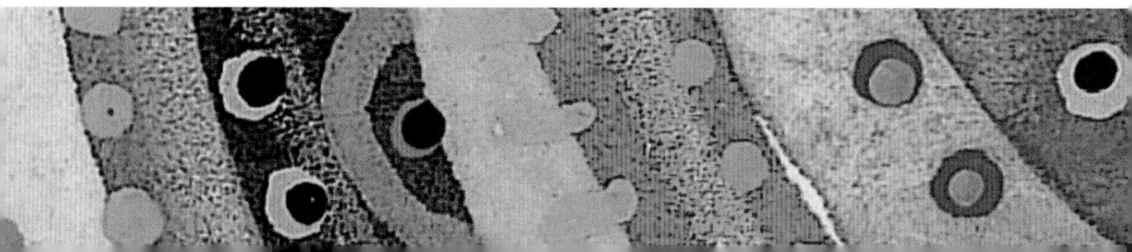

JANUARY 25

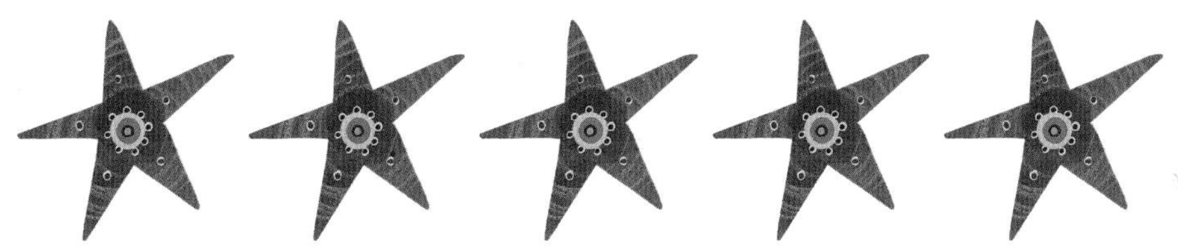

When you commit yourself 100 per cent,
then everything else becomes secondary, really...
The commitment and determination to be the best
that I can be – that's what's driven me on.

SIR CHRIS HOY, B. 1976

Always be a first-rate
version of yourself,
instead of a second rate-version
of somebody else.

JUDY GARLAND 1922 – 1969

You miss
a hundred percent
of the shots
you never take.

WAYNE GRETZKY, B. 1961

Everyone has inside them a piece of good news.
The good news is you don't know how great you can be.
How much you can love!
What you can accomplish!
And what your potential is!

ANNE FRANK 1929 – 1945

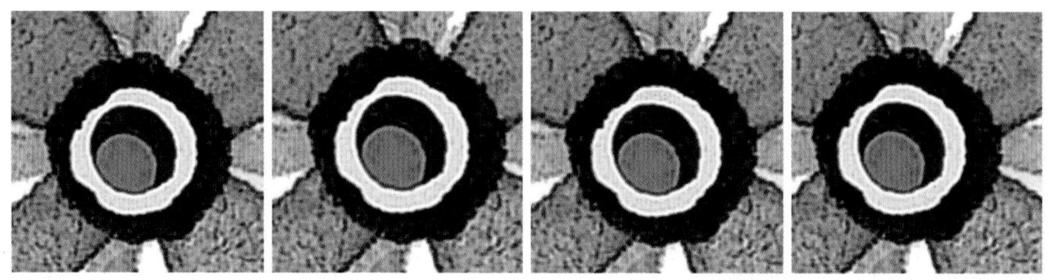

Follow what you love!... Don't deign to ask
what "they" are looking for out there.
Ask what you have inside.
Follow not your interests, which change,
but what you are and what you love.

GEORGIE ANNE GEYER

Strive to make something of yourself, then strive to make the most of yourself.

ALEXANDER CRUMMELL

JANUARY 28

Do what you love, and the success will follow.

HOWARD BEHAR, B. 1944

It is a sign of wisdom to be able to set goals and then, having done so, to let them go. All that is required for success is a vision of the destination. The journey itself will reveal the means that will take you there.

DADI JANKI, B. 1916

Make the most of yourself,
for that is all there is of you.

RALPH WALDO EMERSON 1803 – 1882

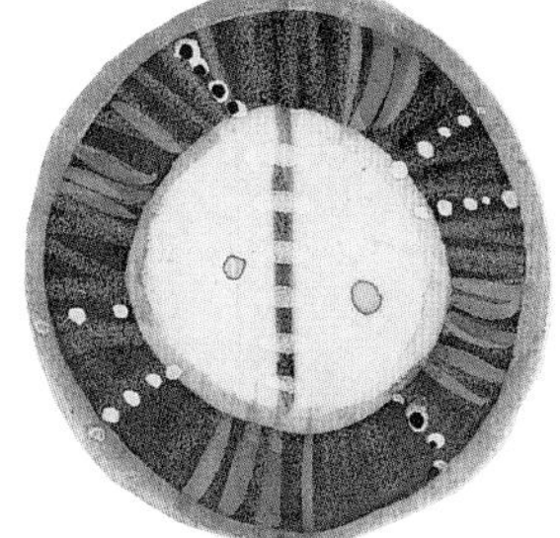

The greatest mistake you can make in life
is to be continually fearing that you will make one.

ELBERT HUBBARD 1856 – 1915

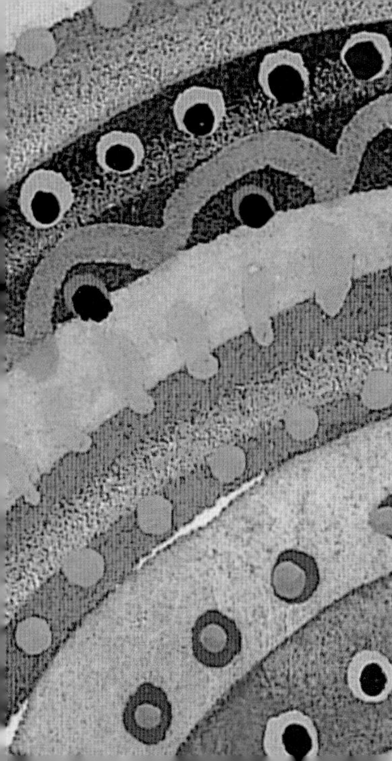

One can never consent to creep when one feels an impulse to soar.

HELEN KELLER 1880 – 1968

ALWAYS LIVE YOUR DREAMS.

MIKE CLARE, B. 1955

It's a very short trip. While alive, live!

MALCOLM S. FORBES 1919 – 1990

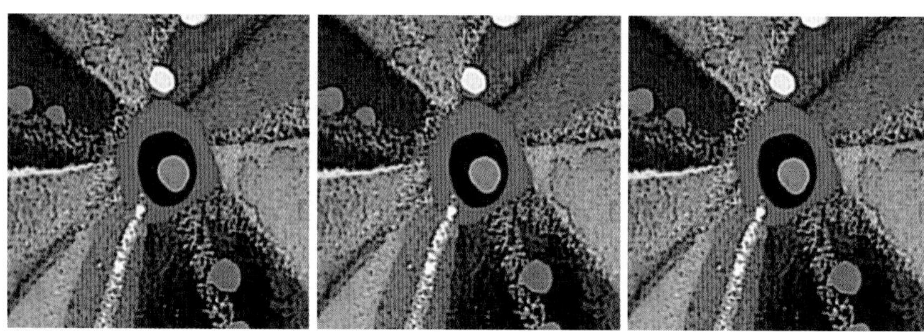

Do not act as if you had ten thousand years to throw away. Death stands at your elbow. Be good for something, while you live and it is in your power.

MARCUS AURELIUS 121 – 180

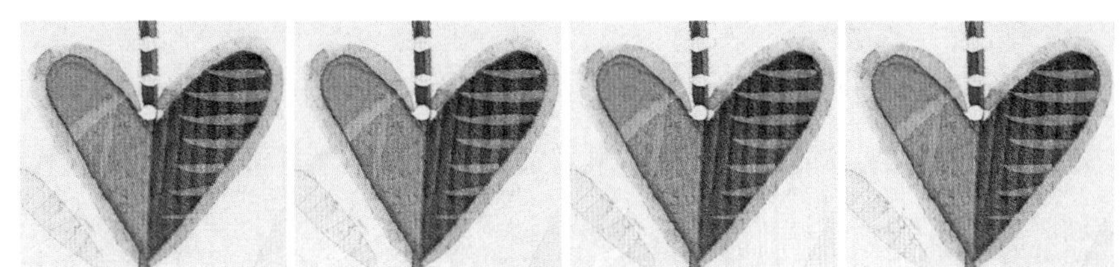

Don't settle for small improvements or little plans,
they're no use to anyone. Make big plans.
No, massive plans. Aim higher than you almost dare.
Paint as big a picture as you can for your future.
Then set about making it come true.

DR. DALTON EXLEY

DECEMBER 1

Einstein's three rules of work:

1) Out of clutter find simplicity.
2) From discord make harmony.
3) In the middle of difficulty
lies opportunity.

ALBERT EINSTEIN 1879 – 1955

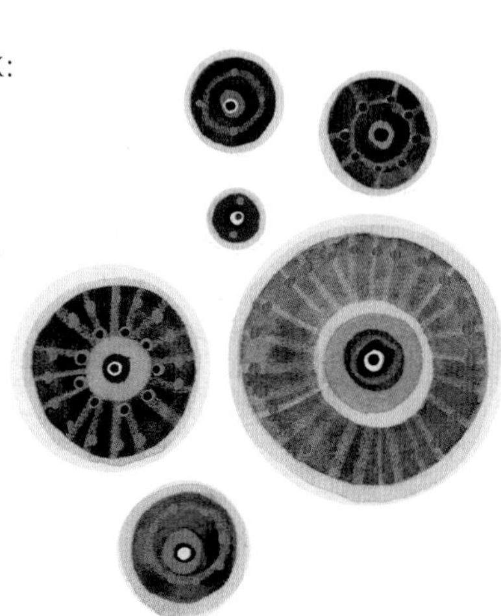

There is nothing more powerful than the journey toward reaching our potential – or even beyond our potential.

HOWARD BEHAR, B.1944

No trumpets sound
when the important decisions
of our life are made.
Destiny is made known silently.

AGNES DE MILLE 1909 – 1993

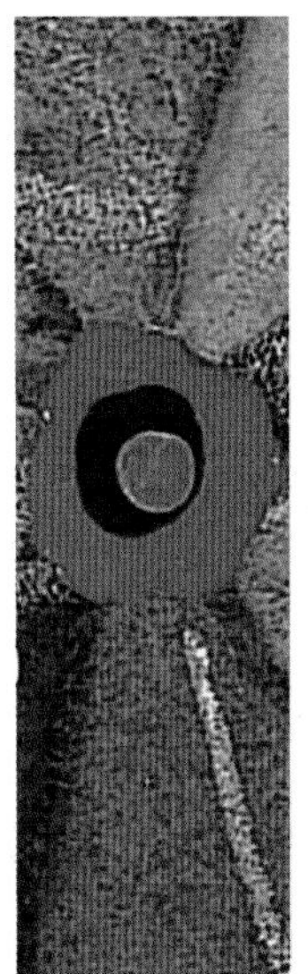

Don't be afraid of the space between your dreams and reality.

BELVA DAVIS, B. 1932

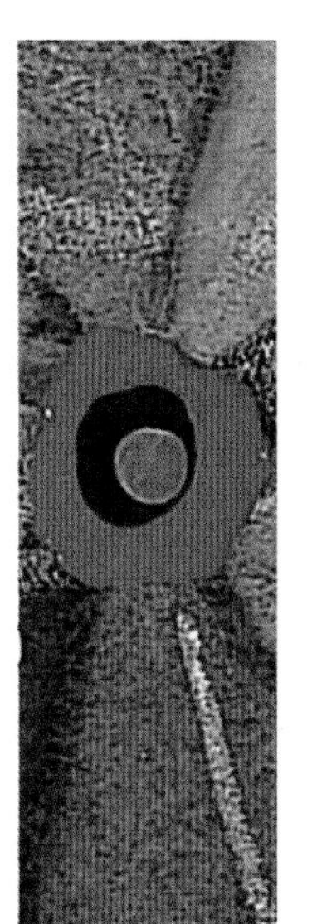

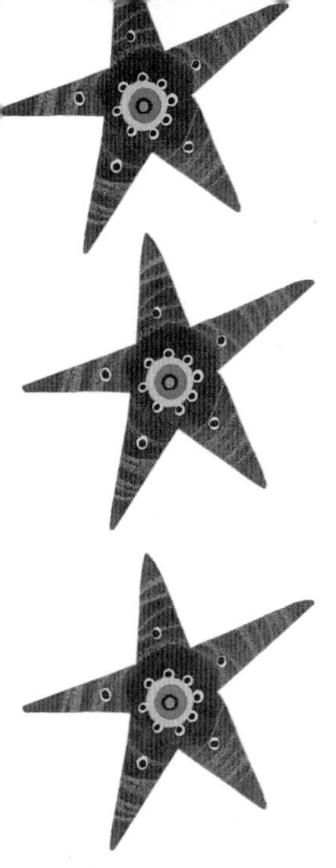

To push yourself to the physical
and mental limits, to ask yourself
to deliver more than you think
you possibly can and to come through,
is the greatest high there is.

GOLDIE HAWN, B. 1945

The day of decision is the day to act upon it.

JAPANESE PROVERB

...for every problem there is a solution.
Even if it means going over it,
around it, or through it.

BILL CULLEN, B. 1942

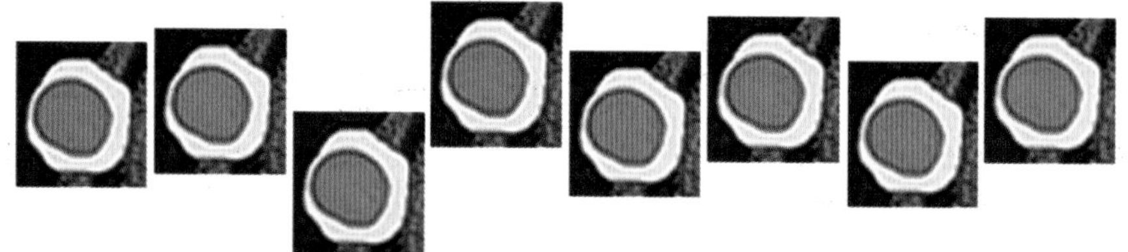

To accomplish great things,
we must not only act but also dream,
not only plan but also believe...

ANATOLE FRANCE 1844 – 1924

The one sure thing that all of us know in life is that it's going to end. So embrace it, feel it, discover it, uncover it. Don't just sit there miserable, making everyone around you miserable. Don't just think, "What if?" but instead think, "Why not?"

ROSEMARY DELANEY

Don't listen to people when they talk negatively
about your dreams. They are not you.
Life is short, and people come and go in your life,
but you are always left with yourself.
Live life abundantly!!! Go for it!

KAMALA DEOSARANSINGH

We have to take charge of ourselves because no one else will. We need to know our strengths, find out what opportunities exist, and be willing to risk for what we want.

CAROLYN S. DUFF

We tend to think of winning as coming first in a race or some competition. Winning in life is just as challenging and the rewards last so much longer.
To feel you are living this life fully, just as you have always wanted to, is a truly wonderful feeling. A winning feeling.

DR. DALTON EXLEY

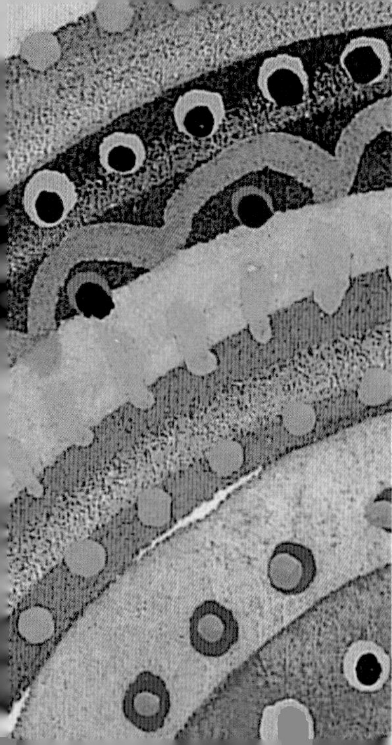

NOVEMBER 25

I must come out,
I must emerge.

RALPH ELLISON 1914 – 1994

If you want to succeed at anything
you have to believe in yourself.

DAME KELLY HOLMES, B. 1970

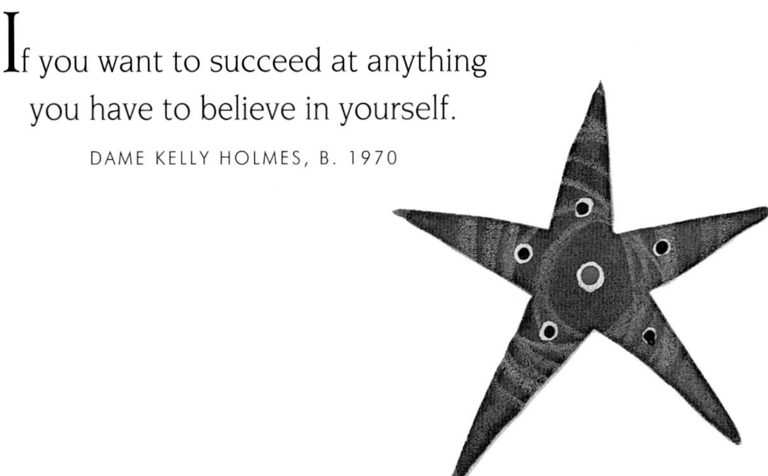

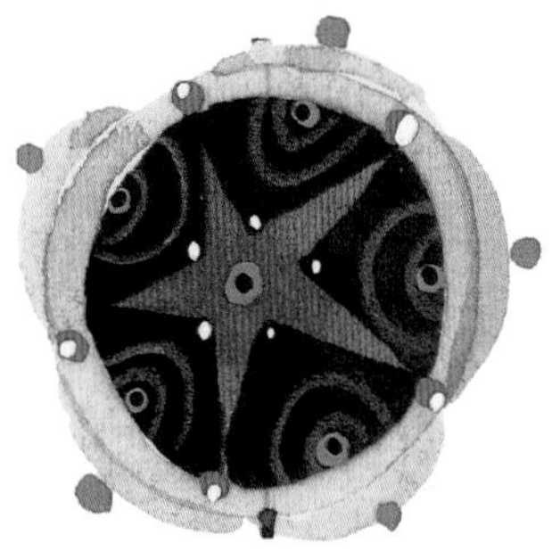

Life is the sum of all your choices.

ALBERT CAMUS 1913 – 1960

How many cares one loses
when one decides not to be something,
but to be someone.

COCO CHANEL 1883 – 1971

NOVEMBER 23

The biggest mistake most people make is to want to become something before they are something. You first have to be something and be it whole-heartedly, and then you can become what you want.

PEARL BAILEY 1918 – 1990

The greatest gift in life is the ability
to think great thoughts and have the strength
to take action so that those thoughts
become reality in this wonderful
and abundant world.

JACK BLACK

NOVEMBER 22

Reaching a goal gives you a new kind of independence because it means that, along the way, you have grown in knowledge, expertise and experience. You're braver, more confident, and have greater determination than you had before.

DAME KELLY HOLMES, B. 1970

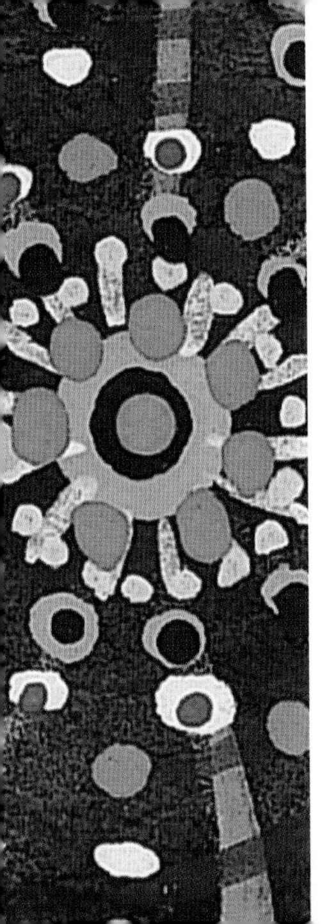

The beginning is half of every action.

GREEK PROVERB

The person who says
it can't be done is
generally interrupted
by someone doing it...

HARRY EMERSON FOSDICK 1878 – 1969

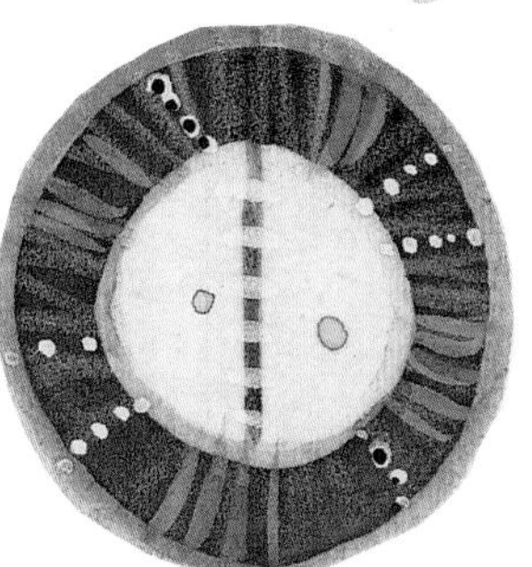

Life engenders life.
Energy creates energy.
It is by spending oneself
that one becomes rich.

SARAH BERNHARDT 1844 – 1923

NOVEMBER 20

Patience, persistence and perspiration make an unbeatable combination for success.

NAPOLEON HILL 1883 – 1970

Take a little time to think about and imagine where
you want to be in five years' time.
Paint a detailed picture of it in your head.
Have the guts and act on it with enthusiasm –
you can make it come true.
You needn't wait five years to start though.
Start today.

DR. DALTON EXLEY

NOVEMBER 19

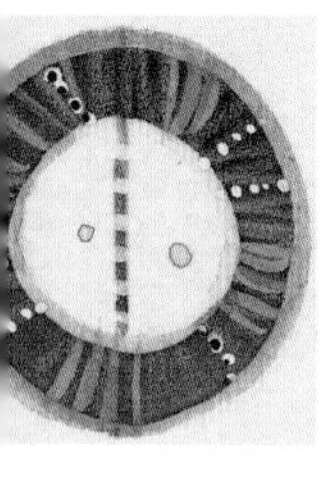
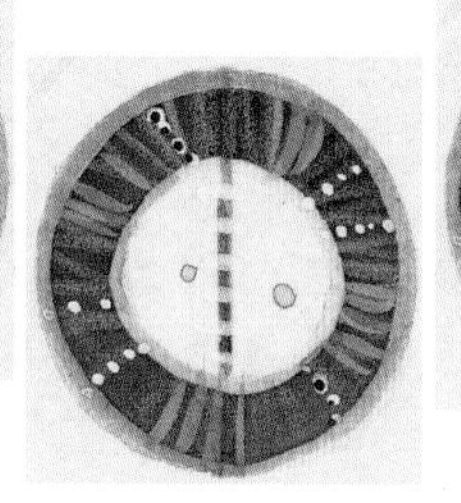
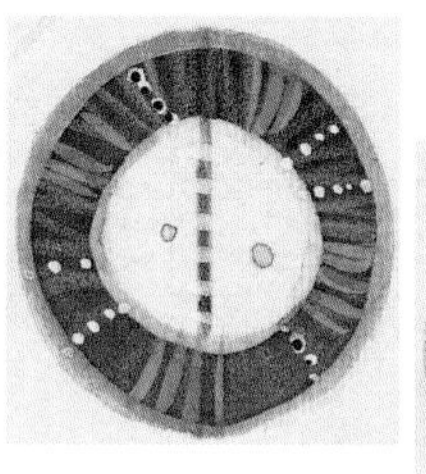
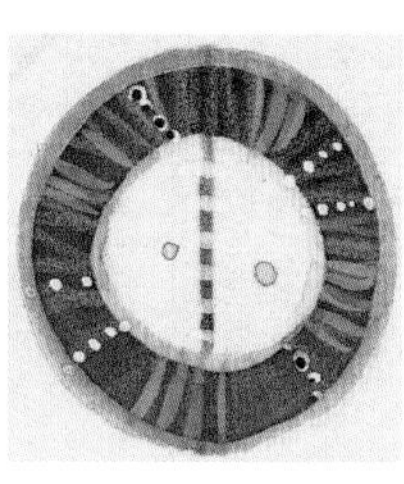
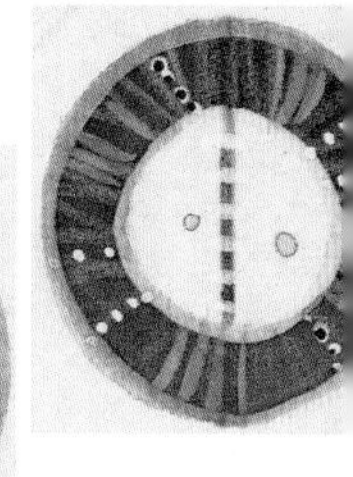

I say if it's going to be done, let's do it. Let's not put it in the hands of fate. Let's not put it in the hands of someone who doesn't know me. I know me best. Then take a breath and go ahead.

ANITA BAKER, B. 1957

The sparkle in your eyes, the swing in your gait,
the grip of your hand, the irresistible surge of will
and the energy to execute your ideas.
Enthusiasts have fortitude. They have staying qualities.
Enthusiasm is at the bottom of all progress.

HENRY FORD 1863 – 1947

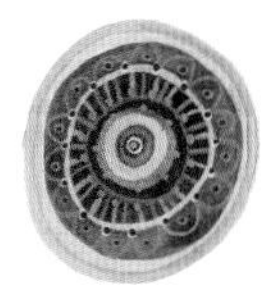
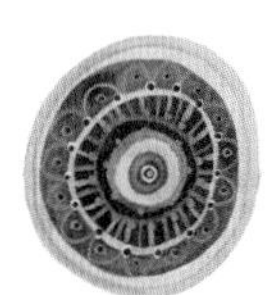
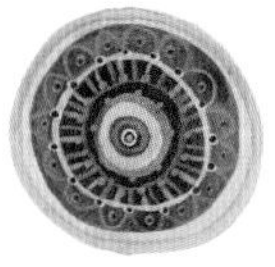
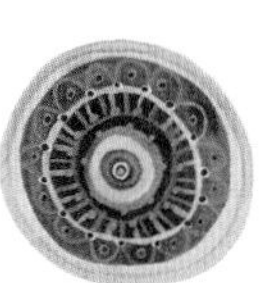
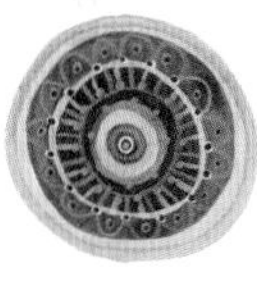
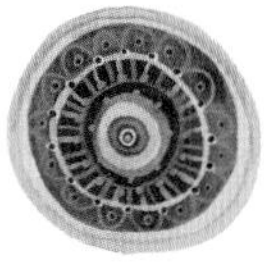

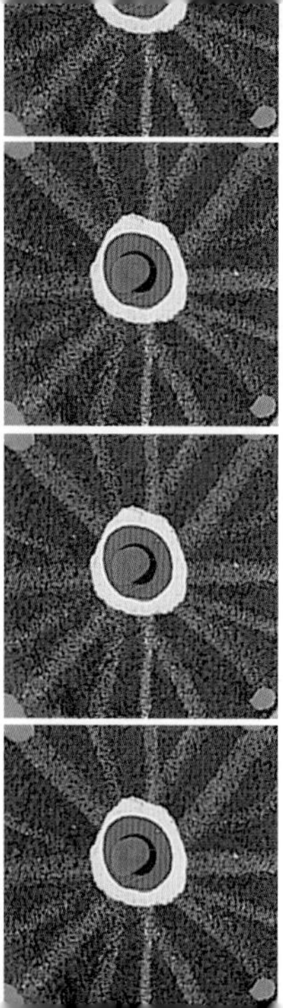

If you suffer setbacks
or disappointments,
you should pick yourself up,
focus on new goals
and try again.

TANNI GREY-THOMPSON, B. 1969

Satisfaction lies in the effort, not in the attainment. Full effort is full victory.

MAHATMA GANDHI 1869 – 1948

The minute that "I can't" is said, you slam a door right in your face.

MINNIE AUMONIER

And whatsoever you do, do it heartily.

COLOSSIANS

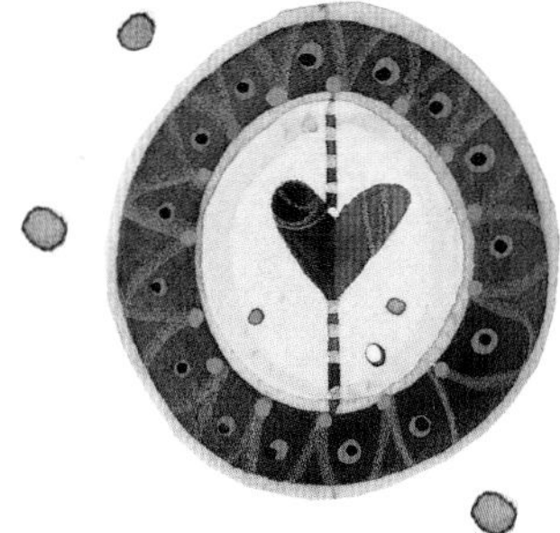

NOVEMBER 16

Effort only releases its reward
after a person refuses to quit.

NAPOLEON HILL 1883 – 1970

Success is not final, failure is not fatal:
it is the courage to continue that counts.

SIR WINSTON CHURCHILL 1874 – 1965

So many great opportunities are open to you – grasp, hold, and by all means make the most of them. If one door closes in your face, try another. The size of your life is determined by the size of your plans. Utilize what you have learned. If given the tools, use time wisely and carve a place for yourself in the big world.

CHRISTINA FORTE, B. 1906

Aspire, break bounds.
I say, endeavour to be good,
and better still, and best.

ROBERT BROWNING 1812 – 1889

The true meaning of life is to plant trees under whose shade you do not expect to sit.

NELSON HENDERSON

Back yourself every time.
Push yourself.
Keep pushing yourself.
Follow your dreams
all the way to where you want to be.

DR. DALTON EXLEY

He started to sing as he tackled the thing
that couldn't be done, and he did it.

EDGAR A. GUEST 1881 – 1959

FEBRUARY 20

A good goal is like
a strenuous exercise –
it makes you stretch.

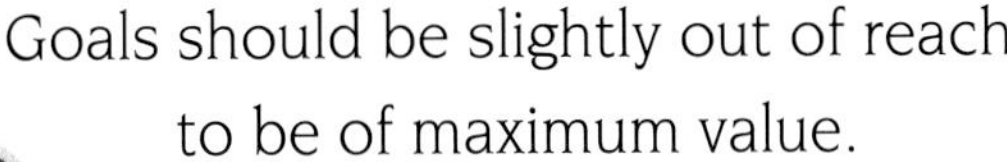

Goals should be slightly out of reach
to be of maximum value.

MARY KAY ASH 1915 – 2001

BELIEVE AND YOU WILL SUCCEED.

BILL CULLEN, B. 1942

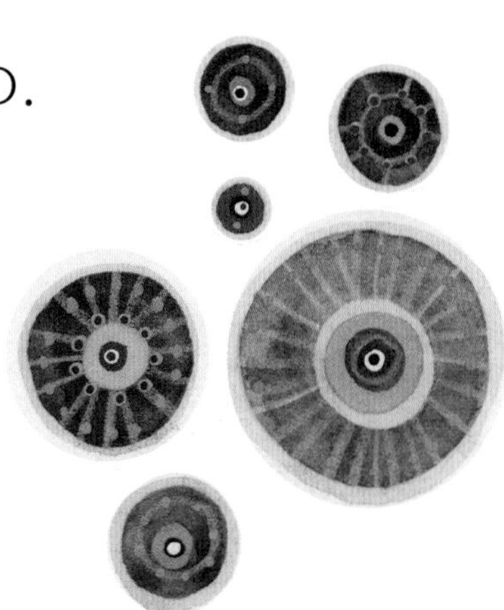

It is time for every one of us to roll up our sleeves and put ourselves at the top of our commitment list.

MARIAN WRIGHT EDELMAN, B. 1939

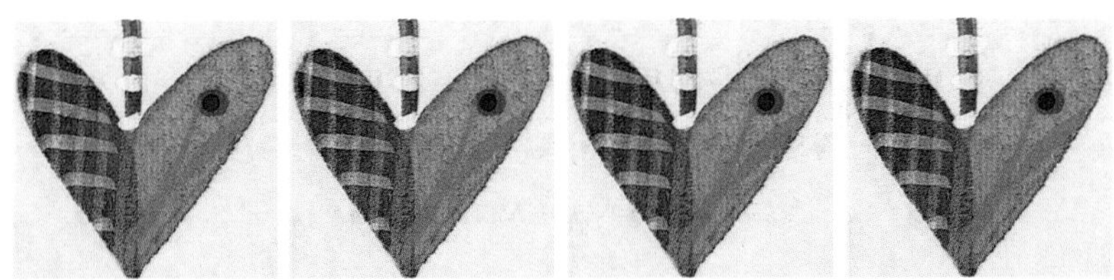

It's not what you start in life,
it's what you finish.

KATHARINE HEPBURN 1907 – 2003

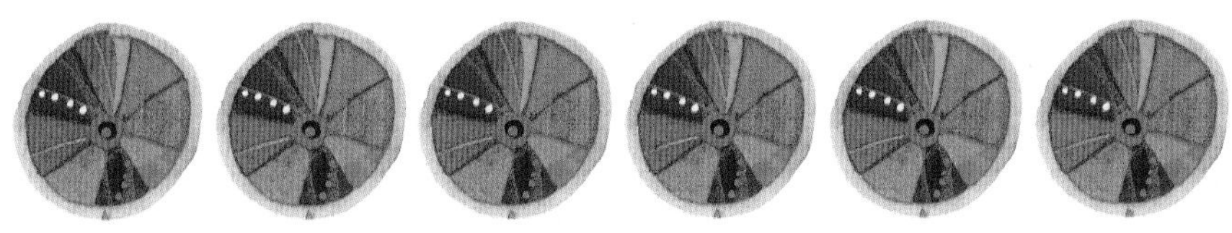

Live your dreams; don't let your dreams outlive you.

DAME KELLY HOLMES, B. 1970

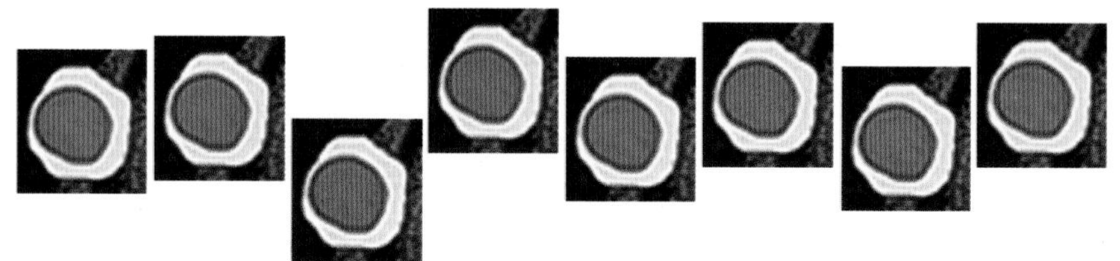

Each handicap is like a hurdle in a steeplechase, and when you ride up to it, if you throw your heart over, the horse will go along too.

LAURENCE BIXBY

Every year I live I am more convinced
that the waste of life lies in the love
we have not given, the powers
we have not used, the selfish prudence
that will risk nothing...

MARY CHOLMONDELEY 1859 – 1925

We don't know who we are
until we can see what we can do.

MARTHA GRIMES

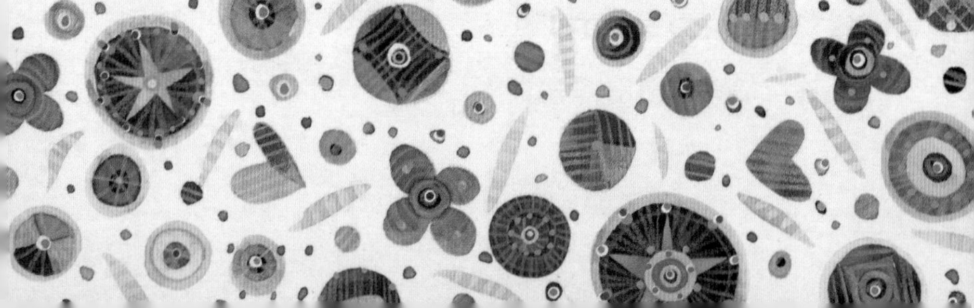

If you practice an art,
be proud of it and make it
proud of you...
It may break your heart,
but it will fill your heart,
before it breaks it:
it will make you a person
in your own right.

MAXWELL ANDERSON 1888 – 1941

Avoiding challenges to avoid failure is a way of guaranteeing failure in the long run. It means a career of missed opportunities, low visibility and low growth. We cannot afford to take the risk of not taking risks!

LEE BRYCE

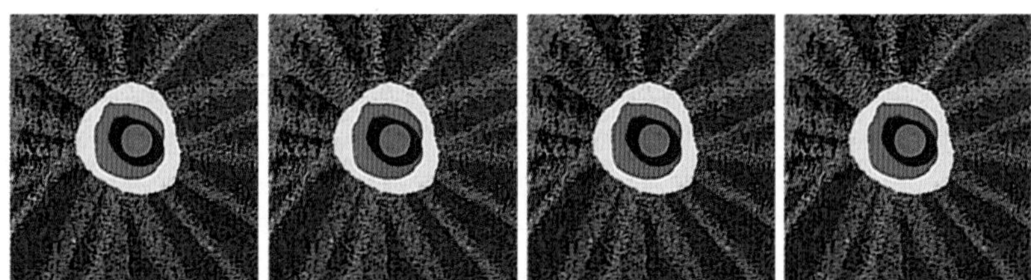

Greet each new day as a new promise, with fresh hope and aspiration. You'll transcend mediocrity and your life will be your own.

DR. DALTON EXLEY

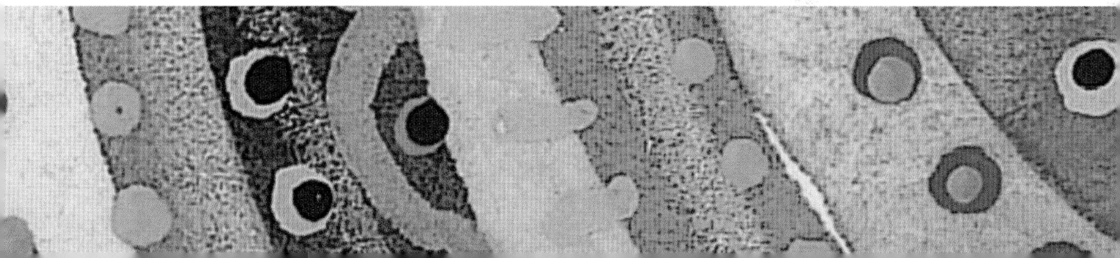

DON'T BE AFRAID
YOUR LIFE WILL END;
BE AFRAID THAT IT
WILL NEVER BEGIN.

GRACE HANSEN

If you think you can, you can.
And if you think you can't, you're right.

MARY KAY ASH 1915 – 2001

No age or time of life, no position or circumstance, has a monopoly on success. Any age is the right age to start doing!

RALPH GERARD 1900 – 1974

Never be put off by things
that are seemingly put in your way,
don't take no for an answer and above all,
make things happen.

LINDA DE COSSART

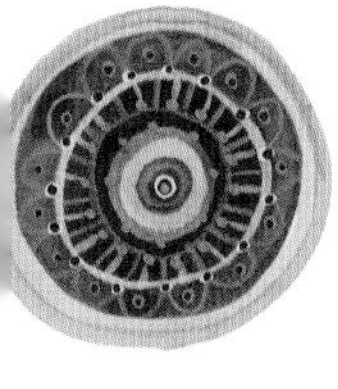
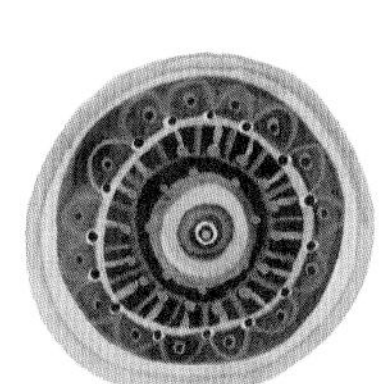
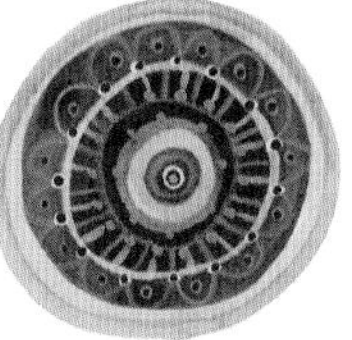
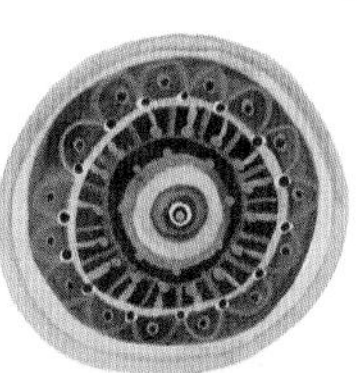
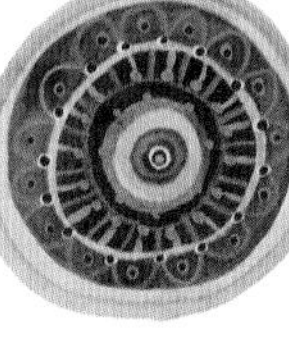

If you cannot give 100 per cent,
then be prepared to be disappointed.

SARAH BRIGHTMAN, B. 1960

FEBRUARY 28/29

Every really new idea looks crazy at first.

ALFRED NORTH WHITEHEAD 1861 – 1947

They can conquer who believe they can.

RALPH WALDO EMERSON 1803 – 1882

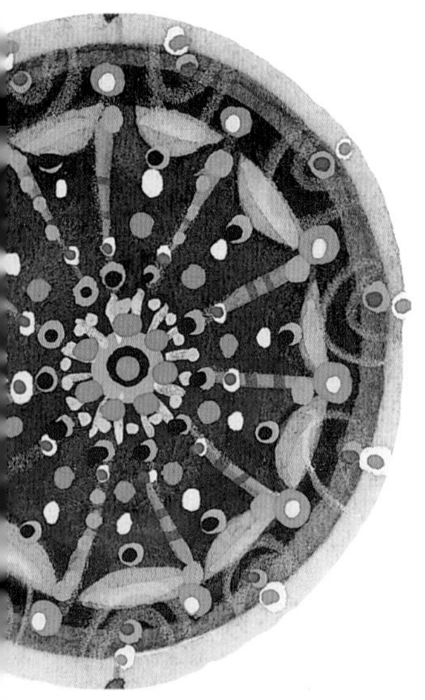

The important thing is this:
to be able at any moment
to sacrifice what we are for
what we could become.

CHARLES DU BOS 1882 – 1939

I've done lots of stupid things, but at least they were my stupid things.

CHER, B. 1946

With life I am on the attack,
restlessly ferreting out each pleasure,
foraging for answers, wringing from it even
the pain. I ransack life, hunt it down.

MARITA GOLDEN

The strongest oak tree of the forest is not the one that is protected from the storm and hidden from the sun. It's the one that stands in the open where it is compelled to struggle for its existence against the winds and rains and the scorching sun.

NAPOLEON HILL 1883 – 1970

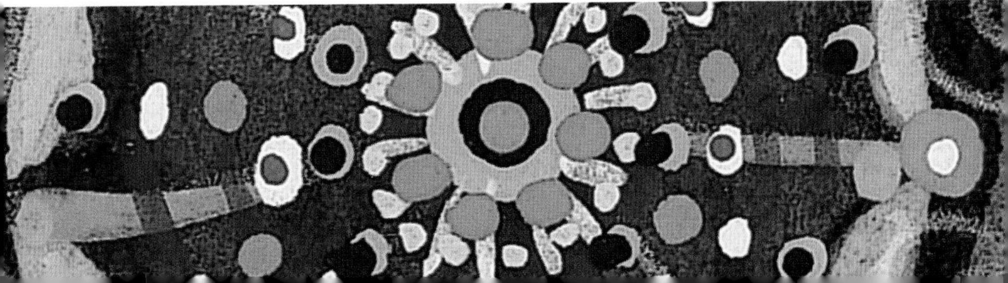

You can have anything you want if you want it badly enough.

SHARON HILDITCH, B. 1961

Hope for better days.
Yes, do. But don't sit and wait for them,
get up and make them happen.

DR. DALTON EXLEY

Everything comes to him who hustles while he waits.

THOMAS EDISON 1847 – 1931

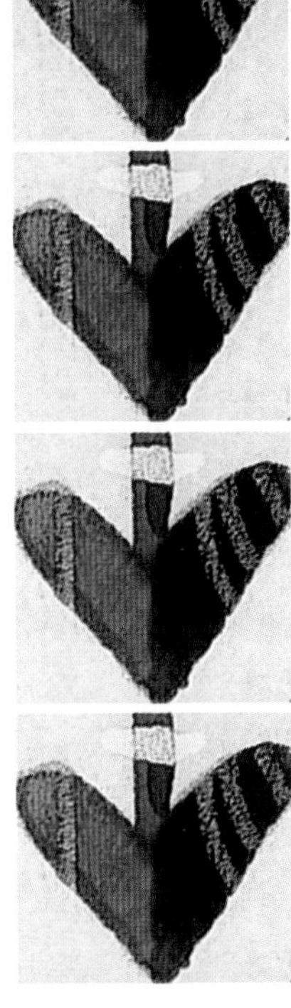

THROW YOUR HEART

OUT IN FRONT OF YOU

AND RUN AHEAD TO CATCH IT.

ARAB PROVERB

I really don't think life is about the
I-could-have-beens.
Life is only about the
I-tried-to-do.
I don't mind failure, but I can't imagine
that I'd forgive myself if I didn't try.

NIKKI GIOVANNI, B. 1943

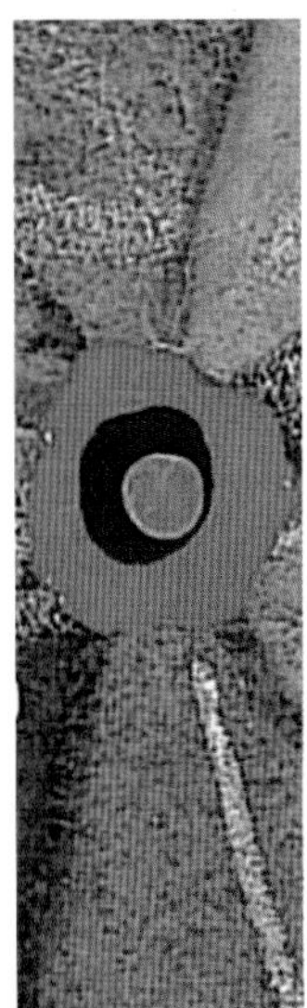

No one can possibly achieve any
real and lasting success
by being a conformist.

JEAN PAUL GETTY 1892 – 1976

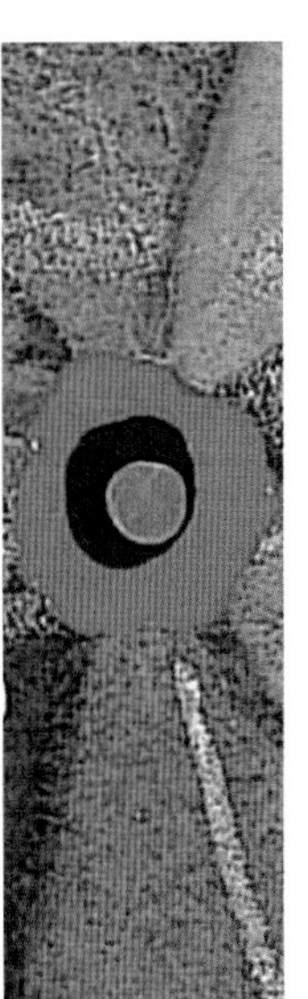

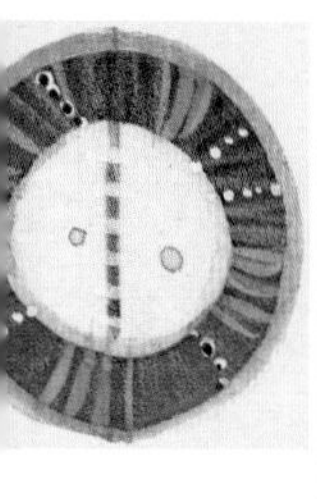
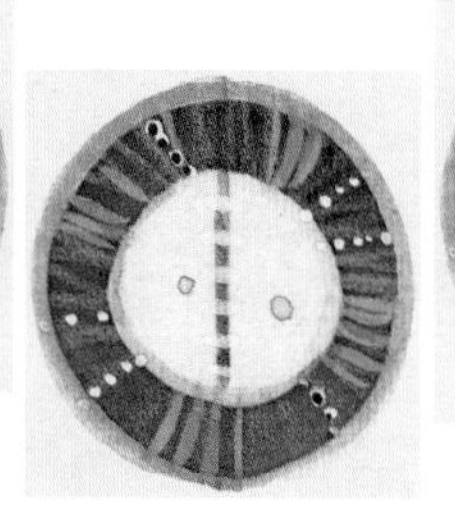
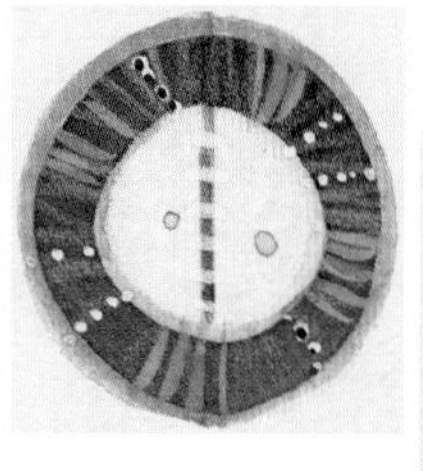
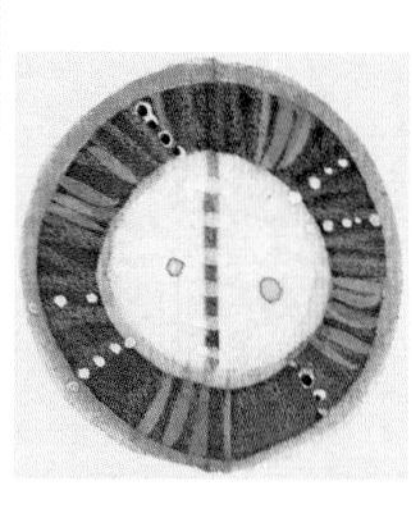
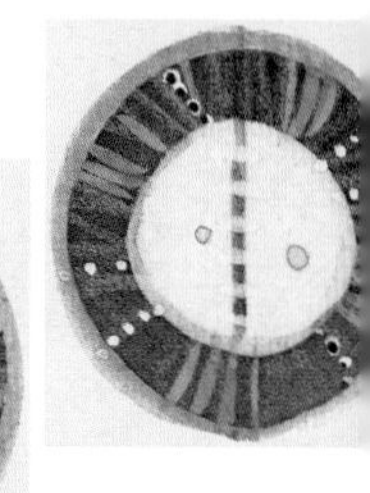

Nothing is impossible if you believe in yourself and you're willing to work for it.

MICHAEL FLATLEY, B. 1958

If you really,
really want something,
and keep a sense of reality
about what it is you want,
chances are you probably
can get there.

DAME KELLY HOLMES, B. 1970

One of the greatest handicaps is to fear a mistake. You have stopped yourself. You have to move freely into the arena, not just to wait for the perfect situation, the perfect moment... If you have to make a mistake, it's better to make a mistake of action than one of inaction. If I had the opportunity again, I would take the chances.

FEDERICO FELLINI 1920 – 1993

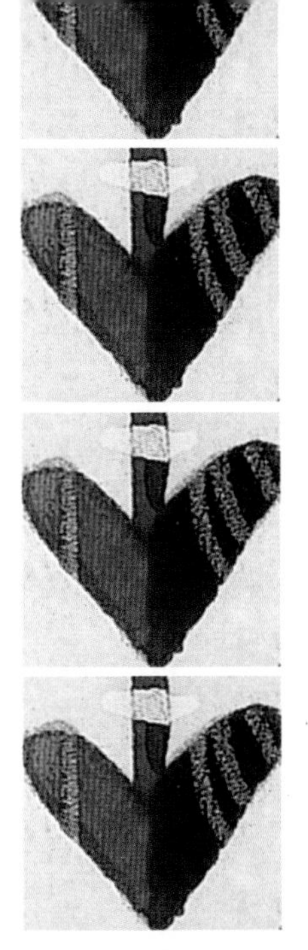

Never live your life on "if only".
Too many people make excuses –
just do it.
At least, if you fail,
then you know you have tried.

HELEN COLLEY, B. 1966

I have always had a strong sense that thoughts are things. So, if you believe you are going to succeed, well, most likely you will.

ROSEMARY DELANEY

It will never rain roses,
if you want more roses,
you must plant more.

GEORGE ELIOT (MARY ANN EVANS) 1819 – 1880

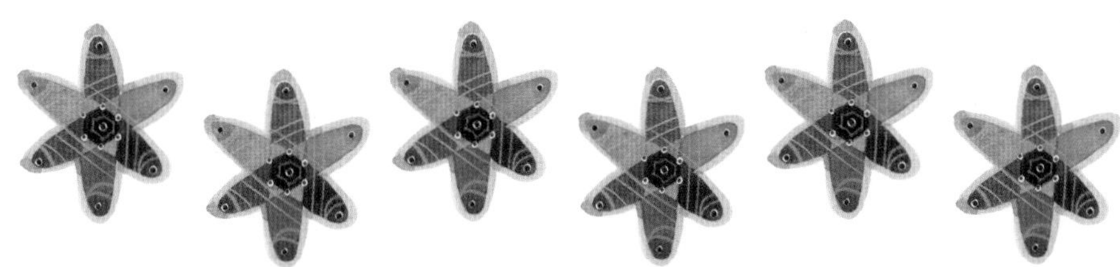

When I'm old I'm never going to say, "I didn't do this" or, "I regret that." I'm going to say, "I don't regret a damn thing. I came, I went, and I did it all."

KIM BASINGER, B. 1953

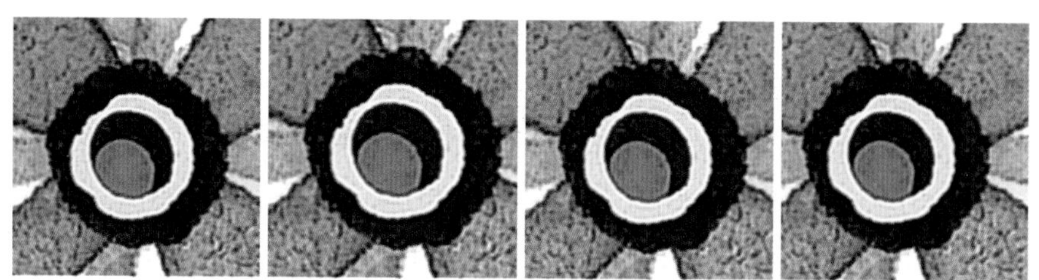

Any successful coach will tell you that a positive psychology or attitude works. So, when things don't work out, be your own successful coach, you have a good enough idea of how these things work. Back yourself, jump back in with a positive attitude and a clear picture of how you're going to get better and better.

DR. DALTON EXLEY

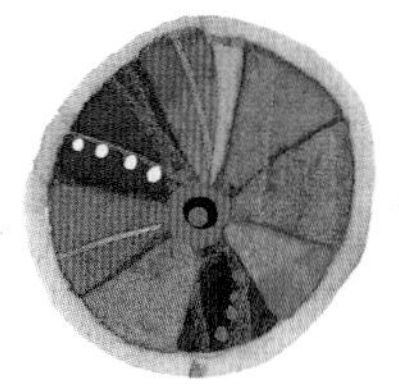
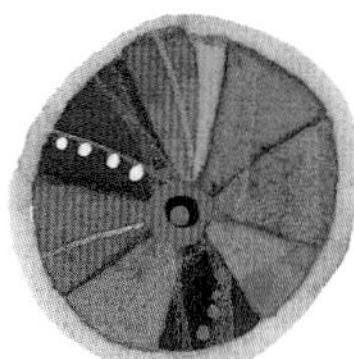
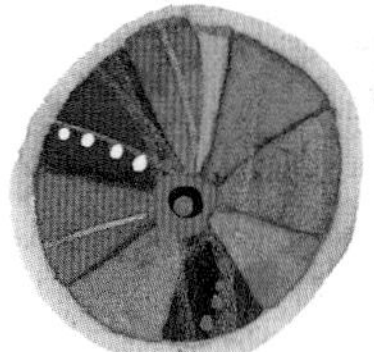
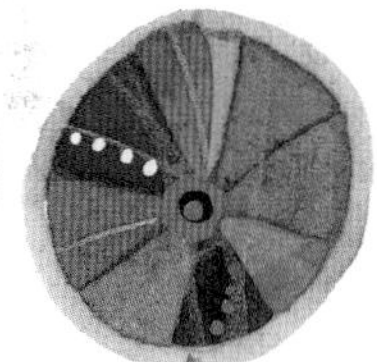

OCTOBER 26

If you are going to do something, you have to do it wholeheartedly with the ultimate objective of winning the race. Nobody ever remembers the person who came second.

RIK HELLEWELL, B. 1958

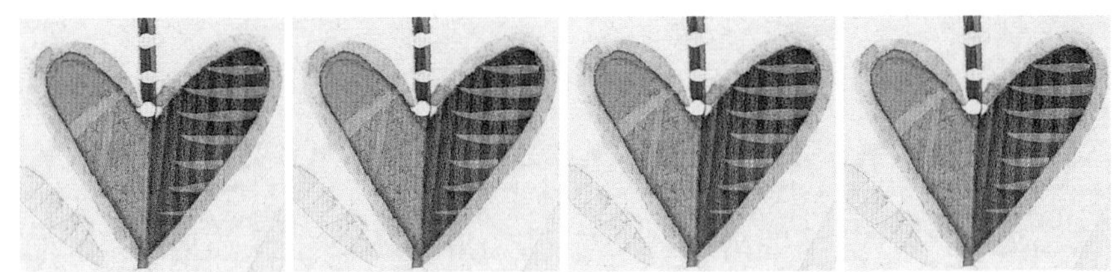

It is worth taking the leap
for something you have always wanted to do
because until you try you'll never know.

LAURA DAVIS

If you first don't succeed,
Try, try again.

WILLIAM EDWARD HICKSON 1803 – 1870

The great thing
in this world
is not so much where we are
but in what direction
we are moving.

OLIVER WENDELL HOLMES SNR.
1809 – 1894

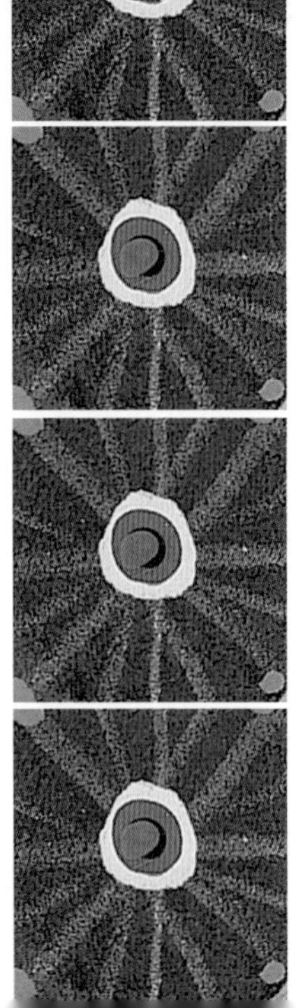

The secret of all success is commitment. No one has ever received, gained, or accomplished anything in life without first being deeply committed to it.

ALAN COHEN

MARCH 12

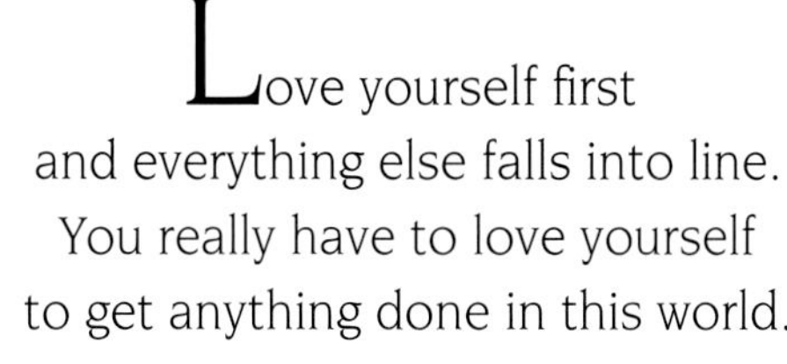

Love yourself first
and everything else falls into line.
You really have to love yourself
to get anything done in this world.

LUCILLE BALL 1910 – 1989

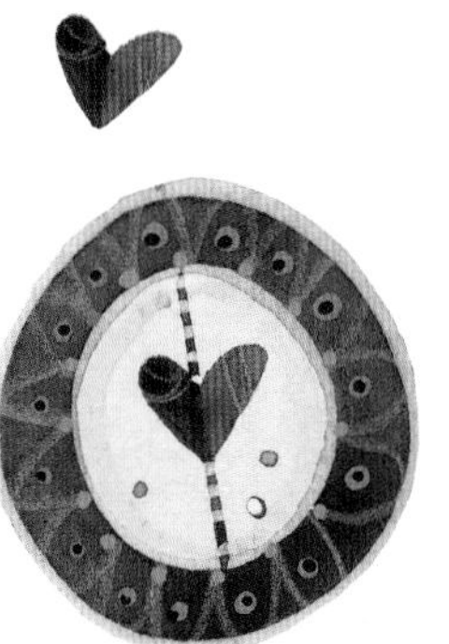

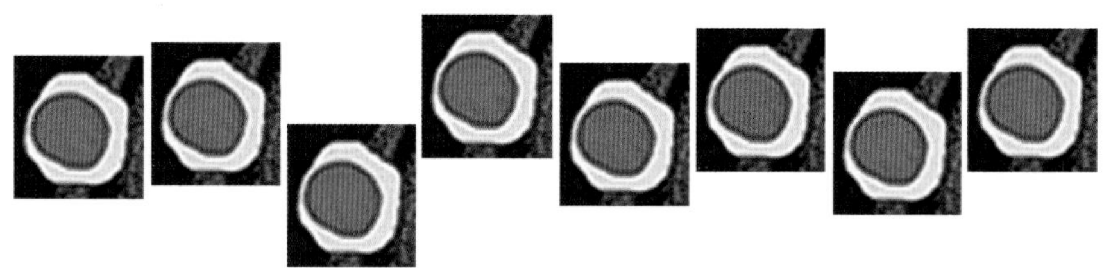

The key to success
is never being afraid to fail.

SUE BARKER

Small victories will get you there, little by little.

DAME KELLY HOLMES, B. 1970

You were once wild.
Don't let them tame you!

ISADORA DUNCAN 1878 – 1927

MARCH 14

LIFE IS AN ADVENTURE
AND WE HAVE TO LIVE IT
AS INTENSELY AS WE CAN.

ANNA FORD

I think it's the end of progress if you stand still and think of what you've done in the past. I keep on.

LESLIE CARON, B. 1931

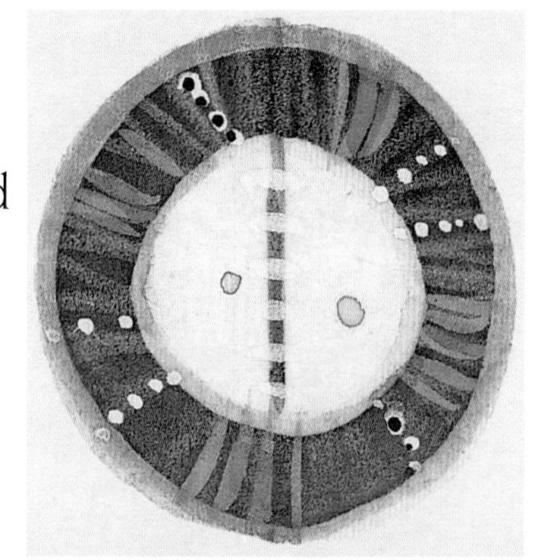

An indomitable spirit sees difficulties as challenges, part of the journey. You can get knocked back, sure, but never defeated by anyone or anything.

DR. DALTON EXLEY

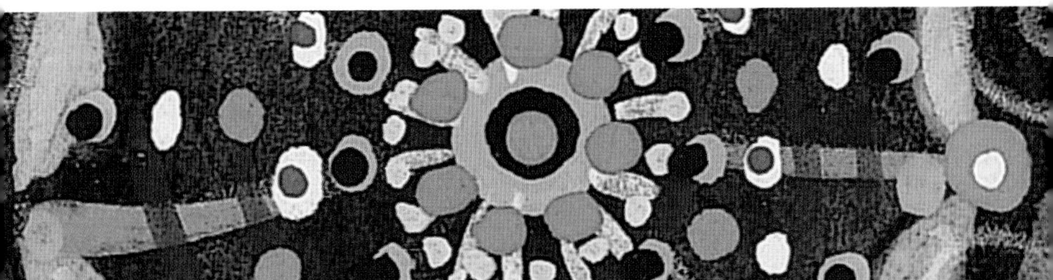

Step into the unknown – live in it – and be prepared to hang out there. We cannot know what's in store for us, and by hanging on to what's familiar we block the new. Until hanging on by our fingertips to the old life, fed up with prising off our fingertips one by one, it simply kicks us into the abyss. As we fall screaming, it prepares a feather mattress for us. Stunned, we wonder why we didn't dive off to begin with. Live life. There's no waiting game. What is it you want to create right now? How do you want to be? Do it now.

CARON KEATING 1962 – 2004

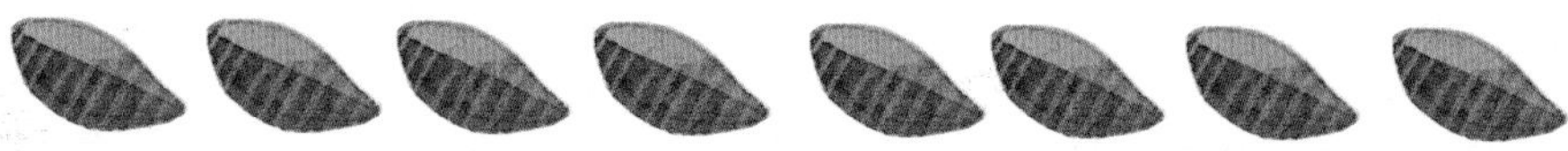

MARCH 16

You can't do anything about the length of your life, but you can do something about its width and depth.

EVAN ESAR 1899 – 1995

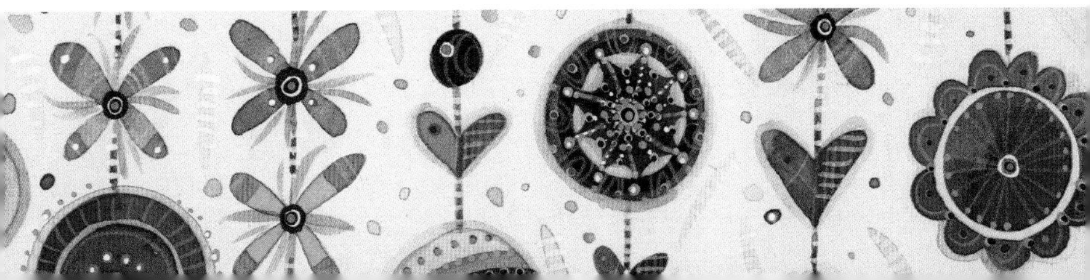

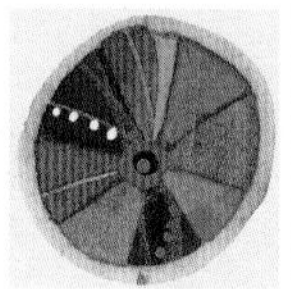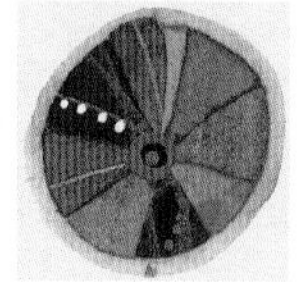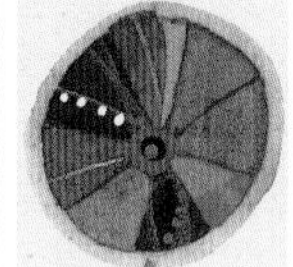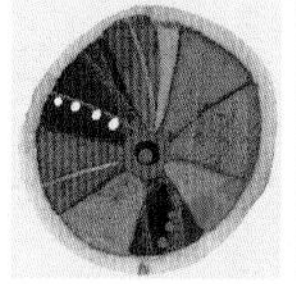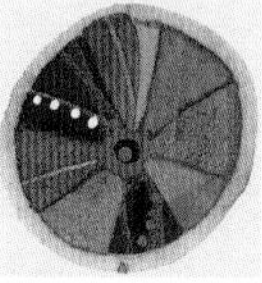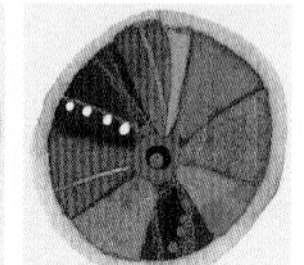

Do foolish things
but do them with enthusiasm.

SIDONIE GABRIELLE COLETTE 1873 – 1954

MARCH 17

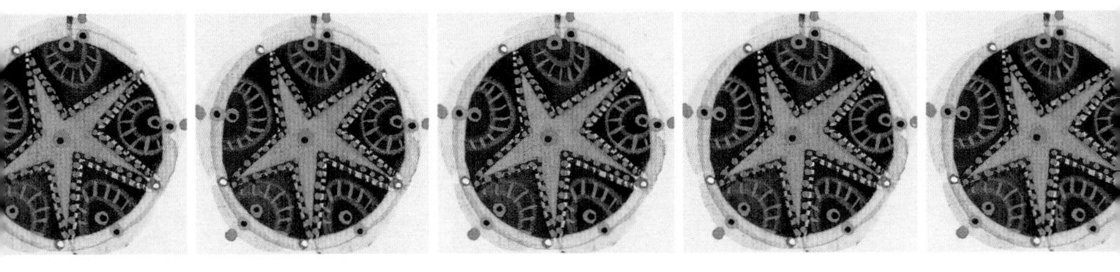

Genius is an infinite capacity
for taking life by the scruff of the neck.

KATHARINE HEPBURN 1907 – 2003

It is our duty as men and women to proceed as though limits to our abilities do not exist.

PIERRE TEILHARD DE CHARDIN
1881 – 1955

Don't let anyone steal your dreams.
Follow your heart, no matter what.

JACK CANFIELD

I found that I could find the energy...
that I could find the determination to keep on going.
I learned that your mind can amaze your body,
if you just keep telling yourself, I can do it...
I can do it... I can do it!

JON ERICKSON

My only advice
is to stay aware, listen carefully,
and yell for help if you need it.

JUDY BLUME, B. 1938

OCTOBER 16

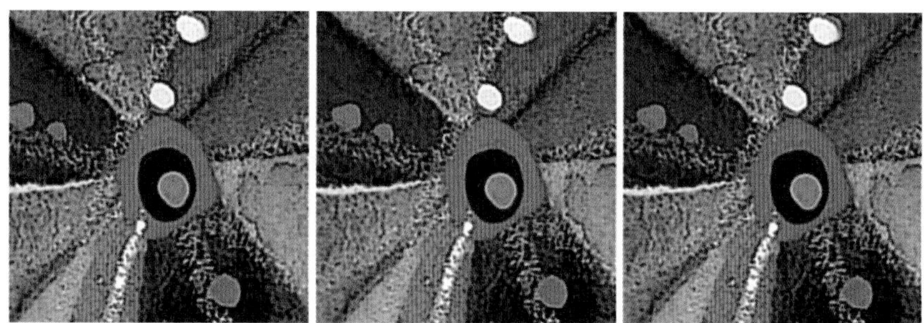

Life is a great big canvas;
throw all the paint on it you can.

DANNY KAYE 1913 – 1987

If you are going to do well in life then you are not going to get any help from others so you have to do it yourself.

JOSEPHINE CARPENTER

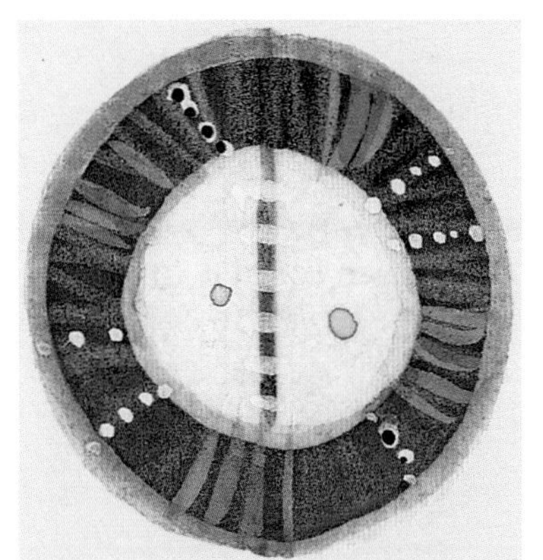

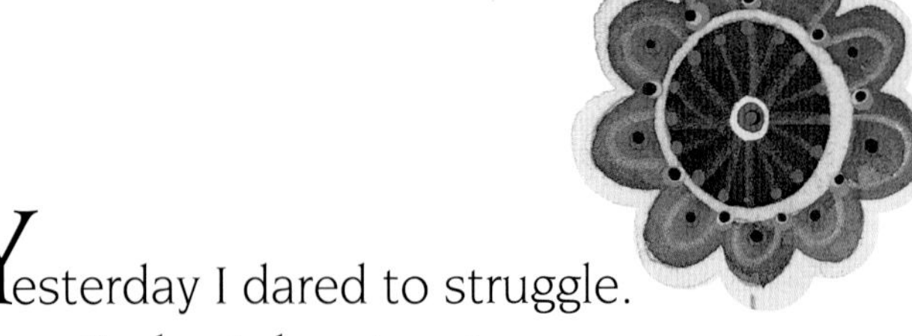

Yesterday I dared to struggle.
Today I dare to win.

BERNADETTE DEVLIN, B. 1947

MARCH 21

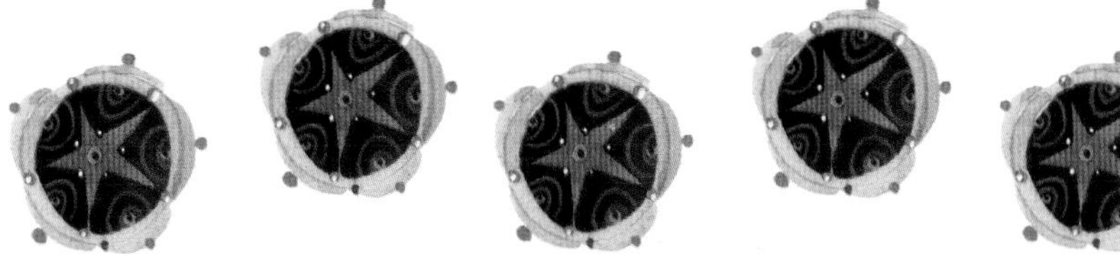

You can spend too much of your life feeling
sorry for yourself that somehow you got the raw deal,
or you can make the absolute best out of what you have
and instead say, "I'm OK, I'm good, I want this,
and you know what I'm going to have it!!"

DR. DALTON EXLEY

Success is the good fortune that comes from aspiration, desperation, perspiration and inspiration.

EVAN ESAR 1899 – 1995

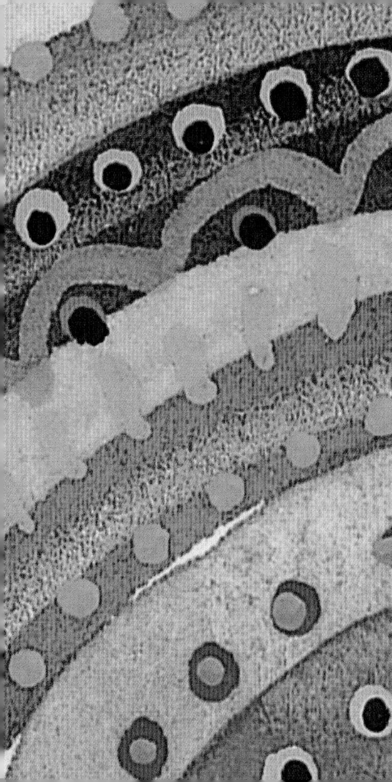

MARCH 22

Achieving a dream,
no matter how big or small
it may be, gives you hope,
direction, guidance, and
often times it can even give your life
a sense of purpose.
And to me, that is a critical
component in living a fulfilled life.

RICHARD JEFFERSON, B. 1980

OCTOBER 13

It seems to me that we can never give up longing and wishing while we are thoroughly alive. There are certain things we feel to be beautiful and good, and we must hunger after them.

GEORGE ELIOT (MARY ANN EVANS)
1819 – 1880

Regret for the things we did can be tempered by
time; it is regret for the things
we did not do that is inconsolable.

SYDNEY J.HARRIS 1917 – 1986

If failure didn't exist,
there would be
little point in trying.

ROSEMARY DELANEY

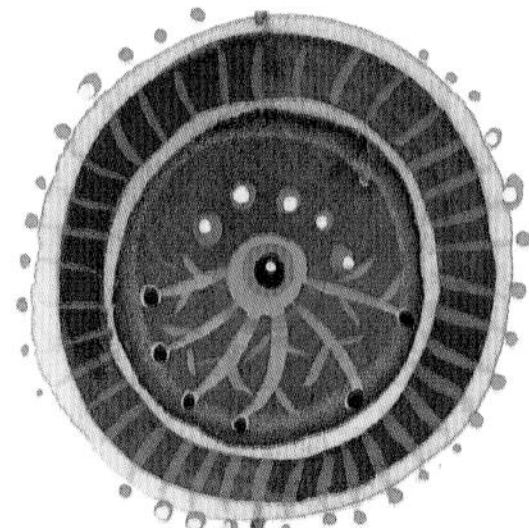

MARCH 24

Turn your negative thoughts about making changes into positive ones.

DAME KELLY HOLMES, B. 1970

If you believe you can do something, you can. There is only one way. With very good attitude, positive thinking, hard work and dedication. With these four things together. If you are dreaming about something you want to happen, it will happen.

SEVERIANO BALLESTEROS 1957 – 2011

In your inmost heart
you must believe that you can succeed
where others have failed.

SIR ARTHUR CONAN DOYLE 1859 – 1930

It's only human nature to want other people's encouragement, but if we're too timid and don't press on without it, we may turn back without ever achieving anything. If we believe in ourselves, it's much more likely that everyone else will too.

FROM "THE FRIENDSHIP BOOK OF FRANCIS GAY"

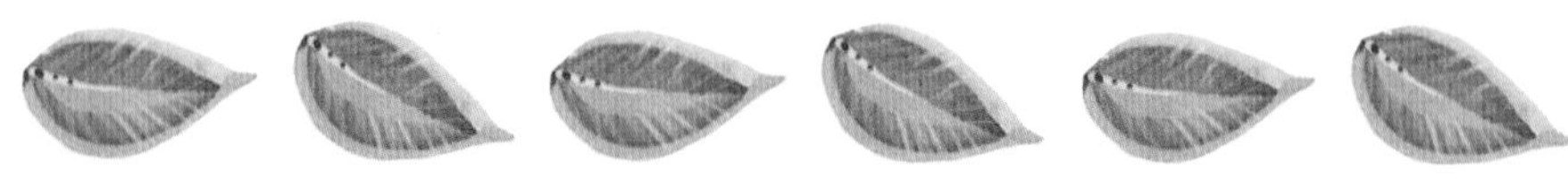

MARCH 26

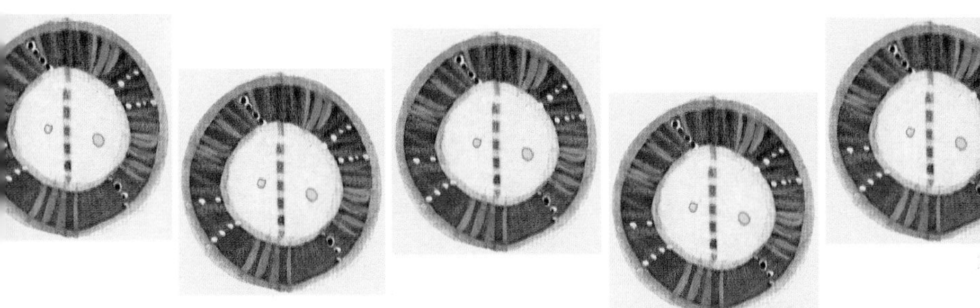

Life is not having and getting, but being and becoming.

MATTHEW ARNOLD 1822 – 1888

If you obey all the rules you miss all the fun.

KATHARINE HEPBURN 1907 – 2003

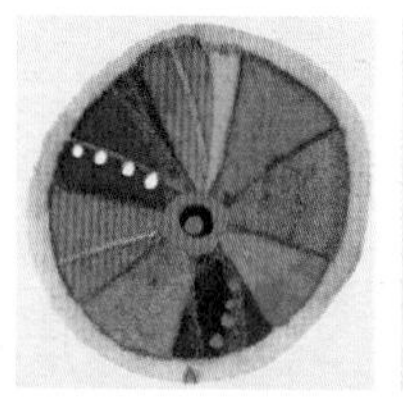
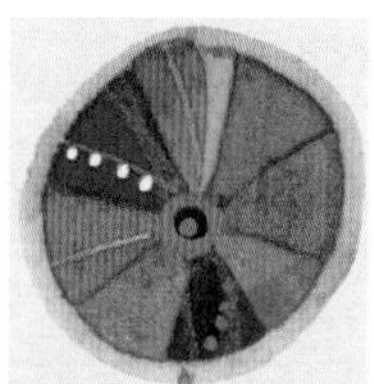
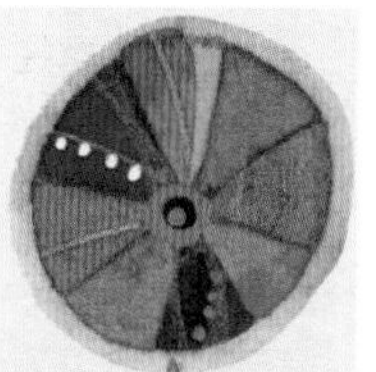
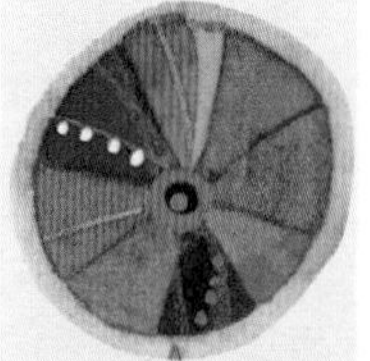

I think the real task is to figure out what it is you want to do in life. If you already know this, and are doing this, count yourself blessed. If you don't, work it out – nothing and nobody is ever going to do it for you. When you know, set about it. If you think you must then read books about it, or set goals, or write out plans, or visualize – whatever works for you. But above all just do it, just go for it!

DR. DALTON EXLEY

Strive to be the best in the world, not just the best in your business.

MICHAEL DELL, B. 1965

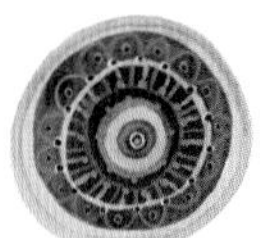 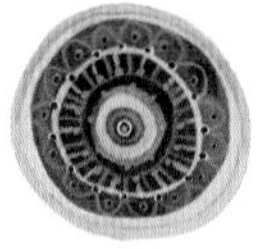 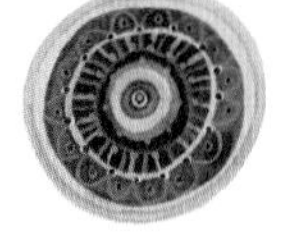 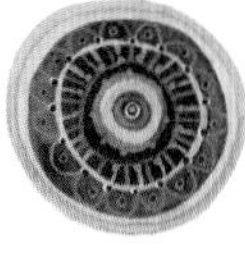 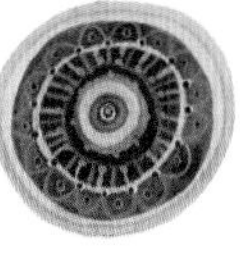 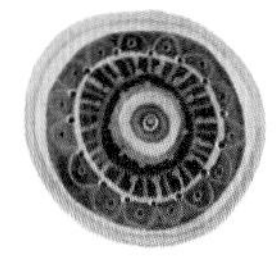

Many people believe that no is the most powerful word in the world... But those who think no is the most powerful word are missing something. Yes is the most powerful word. Yes is freeing and inspiring. It means permission. It means possibility. It means you give yourself and others the chance to dream. Saying yes makes you feel good.

HOWARD BEHAR, B. 1944

Anything is possible; you just have to believe it.

DAME KELLY HOLMES, B. 1970

When somebody says you can't, you come back with the attitude that you can.

GUY DISNEY

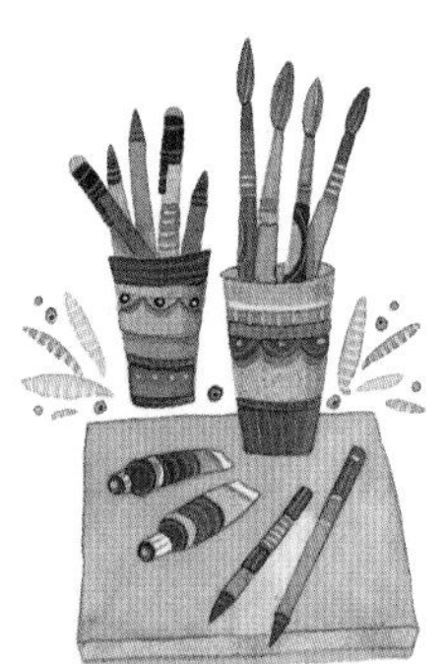

You can do what you have to do, and sometimes you can do it even better than you think you can.

JIMMY CARTER, B. 1924

One step –
choosing a goal and sticking to it –
changes everything.

SCOTT REED

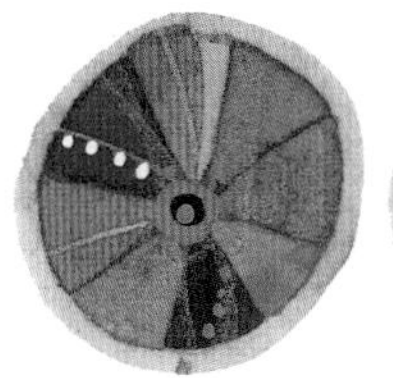 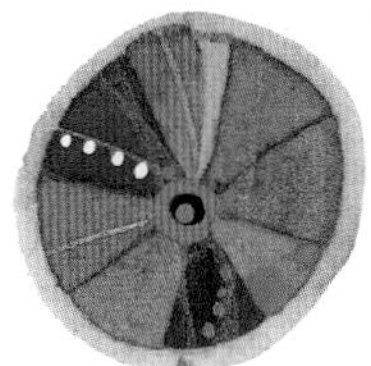 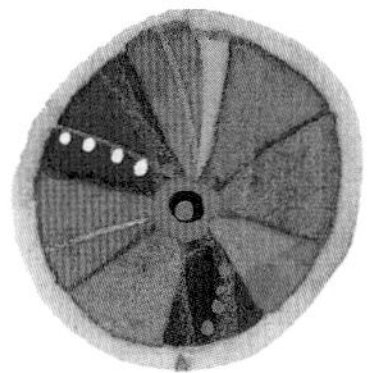 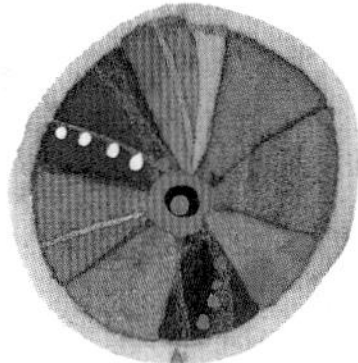

Dance for yourself,
if someone understands, good.
If not then no matter,
go right on doing what you love.

LOIS HURST

Once you make a decision,
the universe conspires to make it happen.

RALPH WALDO EMERSON 1803 – 1882

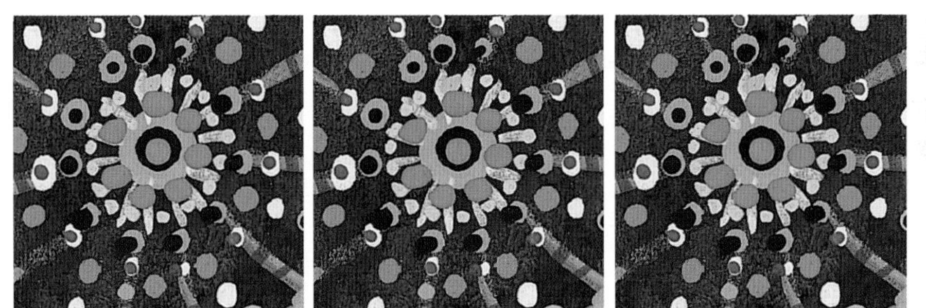

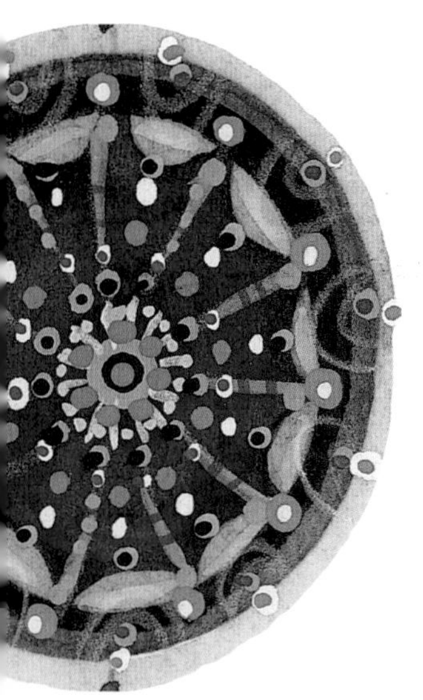

I don't believe in pessimism.
If something doesn't come up
the way you want, forge ahead.
If you think it's going
to rain, it will.

CLINT EASTWOOD, B. 1930

You get what you believe you'll get.
You have to really want it and you'll get it.

BILLY CONNOLLY, B. 1942

It had been my repeated experience that when you said to life calmly and firmly (but very firmly!), "I trust you; do what you must," life had an uncanny way of responding to your need.

OLGA ILYIN

What's the secret to making something happen
in your life? Firstly, you have to want it enough.
Then believe it can work. Then hold that vision
and work out how it could happen, step by step,
in your head, without the slightest doubt creeping in.
Then, and here's the magic ingredient: just do it!

DR. DALTON EXLEY

I should never have made my success in life if I had not bestowed upon the least thing I have ever undertaken the same attention and care that I have bestowed upon the greatest.

CHARLES DICKENS 1812 – 1870

No matter how intimidating
or challenging a situation may be,
hidden within it,
if we look, is great possibility.

FROM "THE FRIENDSHIP BOOK
OF FRANCIS GAY"

THE MEANING OF LIFE IS TO STRIVE.
WITHOUT PURSUIT, WHAT CAN ONE ACHIEVE?

CHINESE SAYING

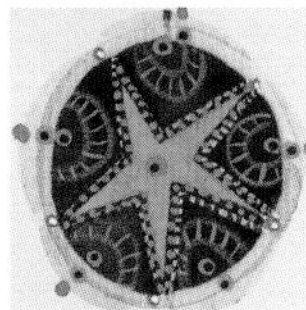

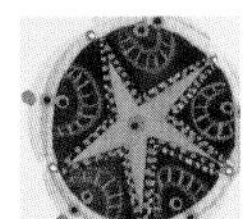

Why be ordinary
when you can be extraordinary?

RORY BYRNE, B. 1961

If you don't daydream and kind of plan things out of your imagination, you never get there. So you have to start someplace.

ROBERT DUVALL, B. 1931

It is not how many years we live,
but what we do with them.

EVANGELINE BOOTH

Press on. Nothing can take the place of perseverance. Talent will not. Nothing is more common than unsuccessful men with talent. Genius will not. Unrewarded genius is almost a proverb. Education will not. The world is full of educated derelicts. Persistence and determination alone.

CALVIN COOLIDGE 1872 – 1933

We often forget
that the action we are contemplating
contains the seed of its result.

EKNATH EASWARAN 1910 – 1999

SEPTEMBER 28

Live all you can; it's a mistake not to. It doesn't so much matter what you do in particular so long as you have your life. If you haven't had that, what have you had?

HENRY JAMES 1843 – 1916

If you can find a path
with no obstacles,
it probably doesn't lead anywhere.

FRANK CLARK 1911 – 1991

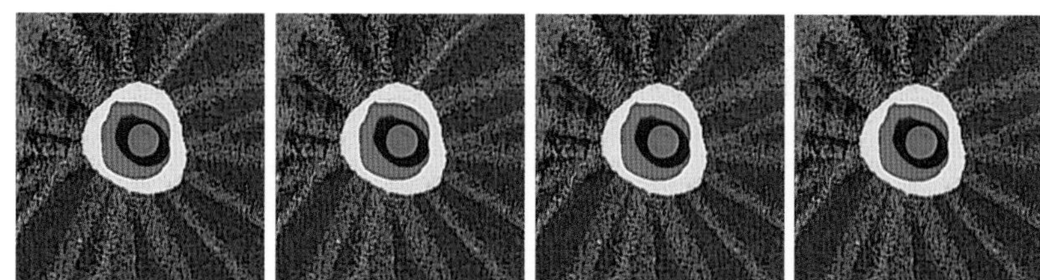

Carpe diem,
Seize the day.

HORACE 65 B.C. – 8 B.C

Hope's highly unlikely to serve you happiness
on a plate just because you wish it so.
It's wonderful to hope for love, success and adventure.
But go and search for them, work on them,
make them yours. Make your hopes and dreams real.

DR. DALTON EXLEY

WHEN WE
CAN'T DREAM
ANY LONGER,
WE DIE.

EMMA GOLDMAN 1869 – 1940

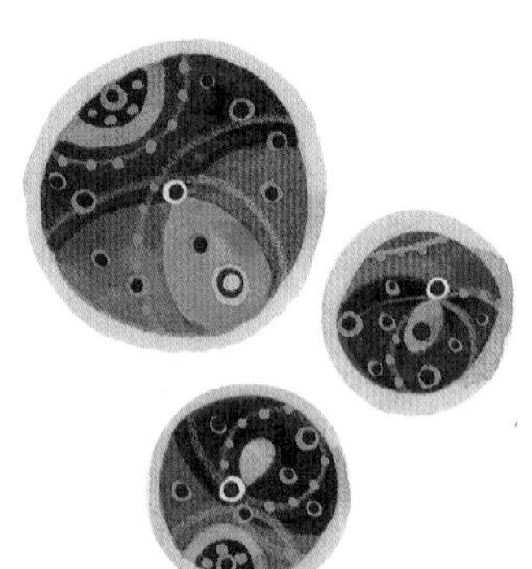

I believe that you must be passionate about your dreams and never give them up.

DAME KELLY HOLMES, B. 1970

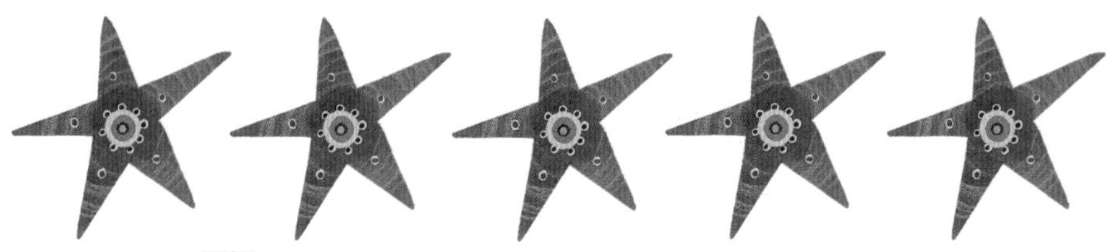

To succeed in life doesn't mean never failing. Far from it, it's not how often you fail, but how you react and bounce back that's important. If you keep on rising back up you will find your success.

DR. DALTON EXLEY

I want to win. That's it, all of it.

AL DAVIS

Do not go where the path may lead,
go instead where there is no path
and leave a trail.

RALPH WALDO EMERSON 1803 – 1882

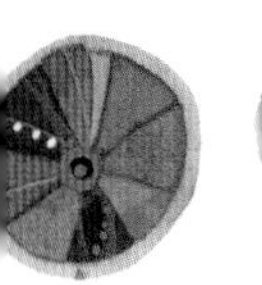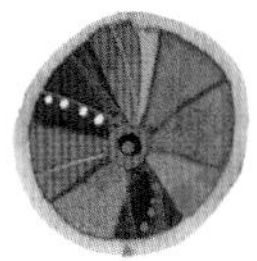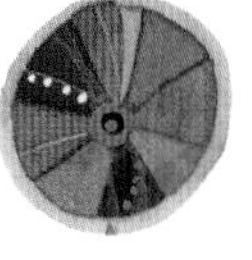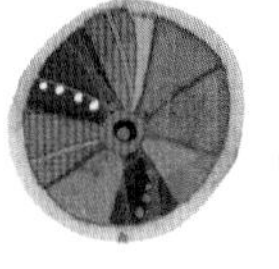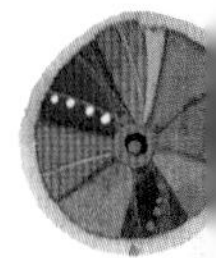

If you want to do something enough
and you have the determination
and will to succeed, then you will.

BETTY BOOTHROYD, B. 1929

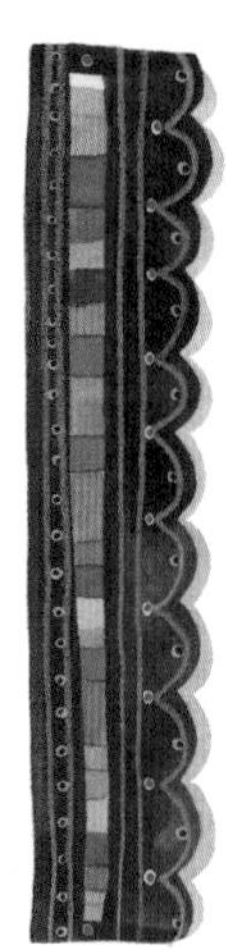

You must learn day by day, year by year, to broaden your horizon. The more things you love, the more you are interested in, the more you enjoy, the more you are indignant about – the more you have left when anything happens.

ETHEL BARRYMORE 1879 – 1959

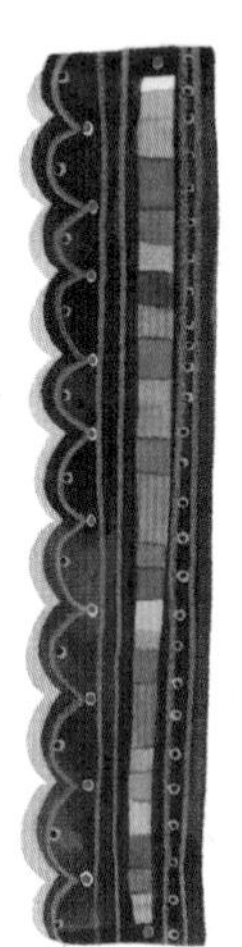

Great works are performed not by strength but by perseverance.

DR. SAMUEL JOHNSON 1709 – 1784

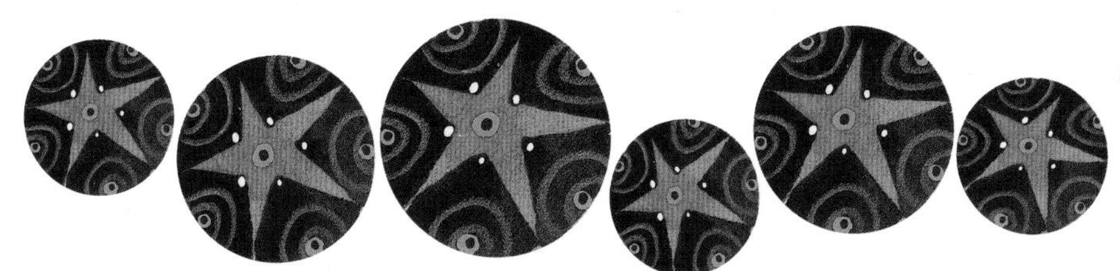

SEPTEMBER 22

Crying over one opportunity missed can cloud the vision you need in order not to miss the next one.

DADI JANKI, B. 1916

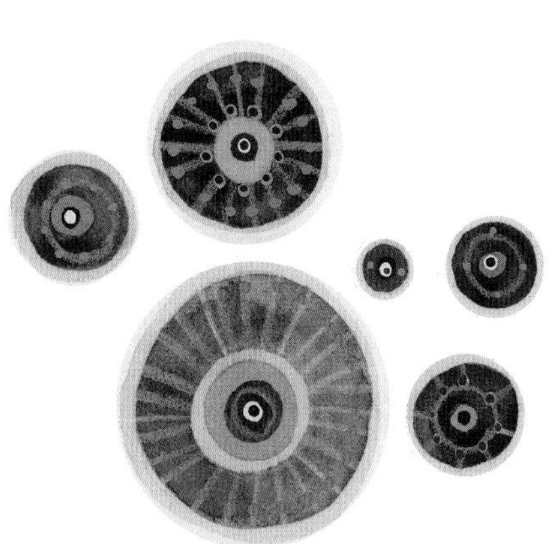

Character consists of what you do on the third and fourth tries.

JAMES A. MICHENER 1907 – 1997

When you have to make a choice and don't make it, that is itself a choice.

WILLIAM JAMES 1842 – 1910

It's great to have the potential to make things happen.
But it's no use if we don't use it.
Recognize what you really want out of life,
where you want to get to, grasp your potential firmly
and have confidence in yourself to achieve it.

DR. DALTON EXLEY

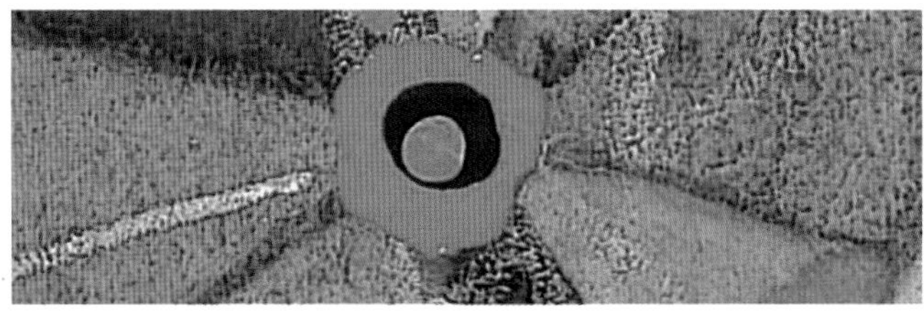

SEPTEMBER 20

When you reach for the stars, you may not quite get them, but you won't come up with a handful of mud either.

LEO BURNETT 1891 – 1971

Always focus on your goal, not the obstacle, and your dreams and goals will come true.

PETER EBDON, B. 1970

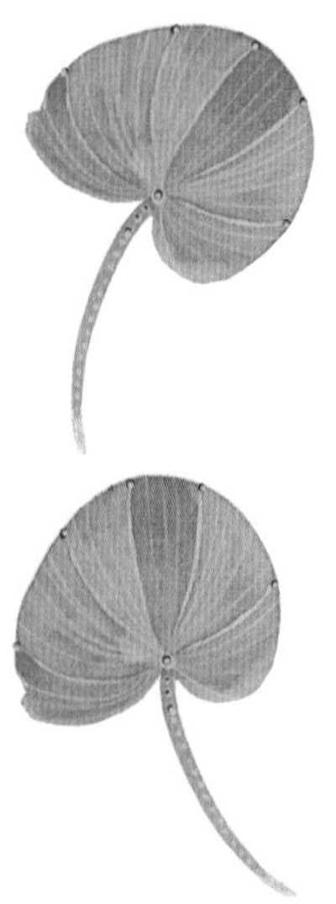

Our chief want in life
is someone who will make us
do what we can.

RALPH WALDO EMERSON 1803 – 1882

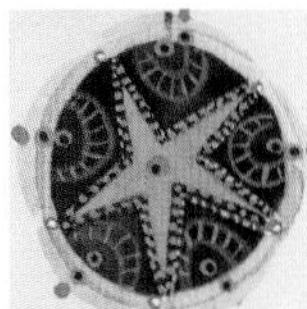

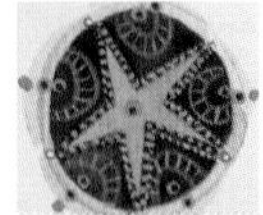

If you do not go after what you want,
you'll never have it.
If you do not ask, the answer will always be no.
If you do not step forward,
you will always be in the same place.

AUTHOR UNKNOWN

...strength and courage aren't always measured in medals and victories. They are measured in the struggles we overcome. The strongest people are not always the people who win, but the people who don't give up when they lose.

ASHLEY HODGESON

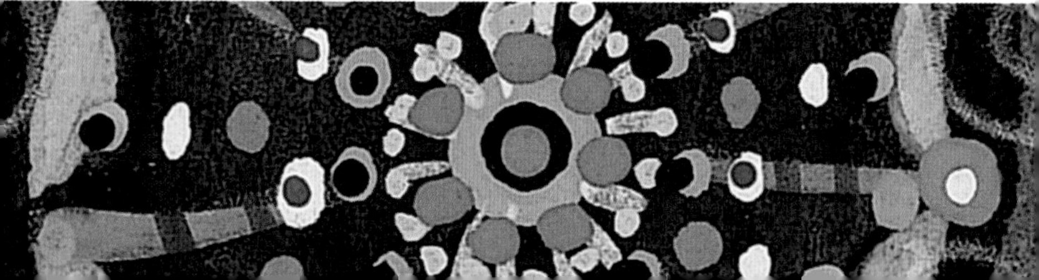

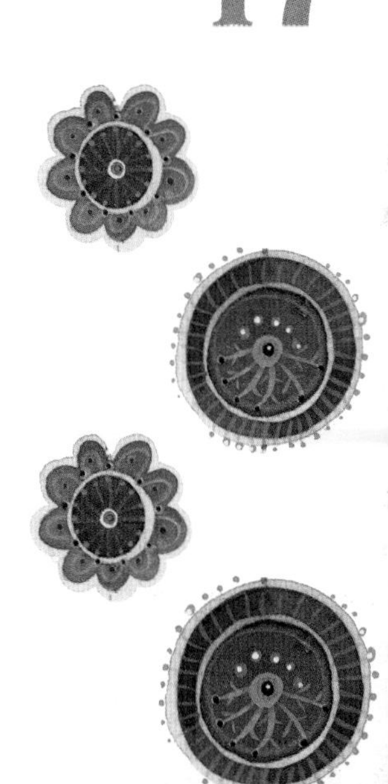

There are three primary principles essential to the success of any venture. They are simple, but important:

1. Determine your objectives.
2. Analyse the obstacles in your way.
3. Learn how to overcome your obstacles.

DICK CARLSON

Seek out that particular mental attitude which makes you feel most deeply and vitally alive, along with which comes the inner voice which says, "This is the real me," and when you have found that attitude, follow it.

WILLIAM JAMES 1842 – 1910

The only person that can stop you from doing what you want is yourself.

LUCY GAFFNEY

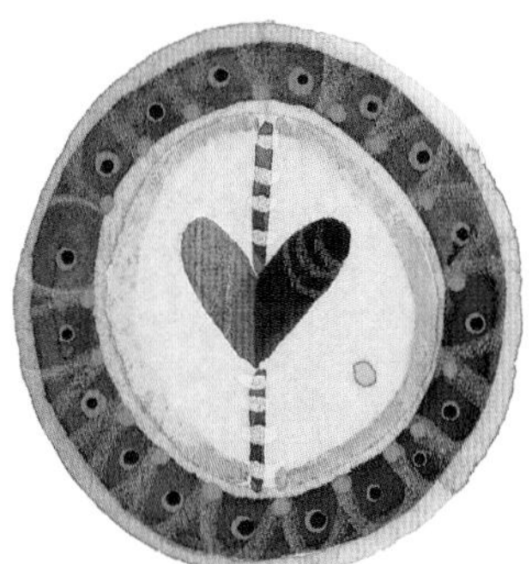

The two important things I did learn were that you are as powerful and strong as you allow yourself to be, and that the most difficult part of any endeavour is taking the first step, making the first decision.

ROBYN DAVIDSON

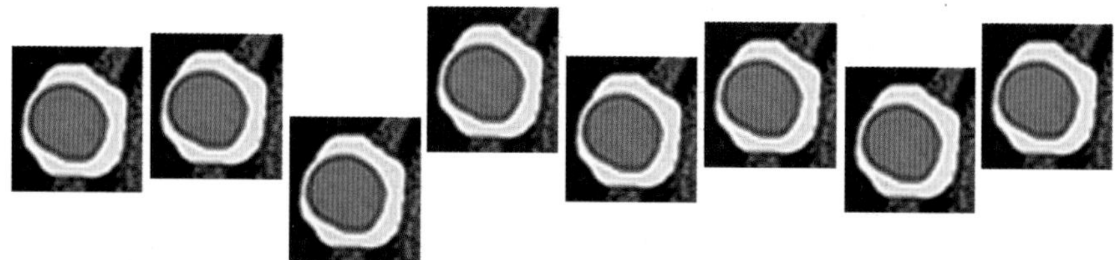

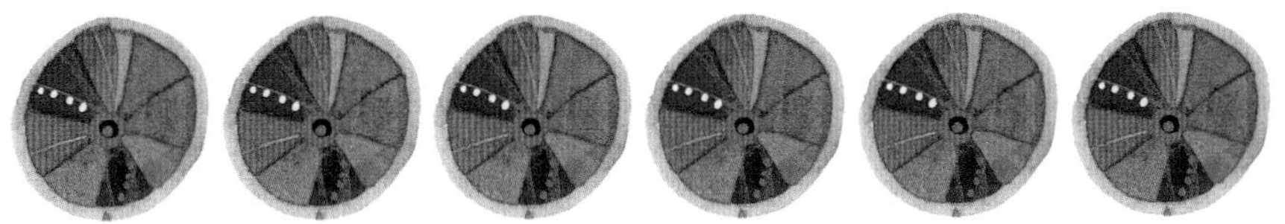

We're born with success.
It's only others who point out our failures
and what they attribute to us as failures.

WHOOPI GOLDBERG, B. 1955

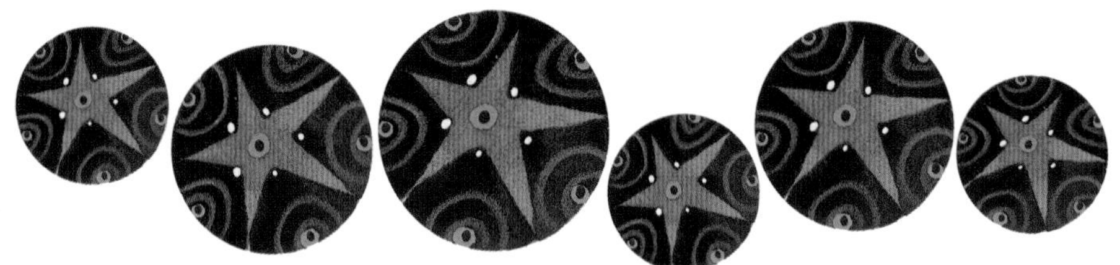

To say yes, you have to sweat and roll up your sleeves and plunge both hands into life up to the elbows.

JEAN ANOUILH 1910 – 1987

To be successful at most things involves taking chances. Take risks. Just go for it.

DR. DALTON EXLEY

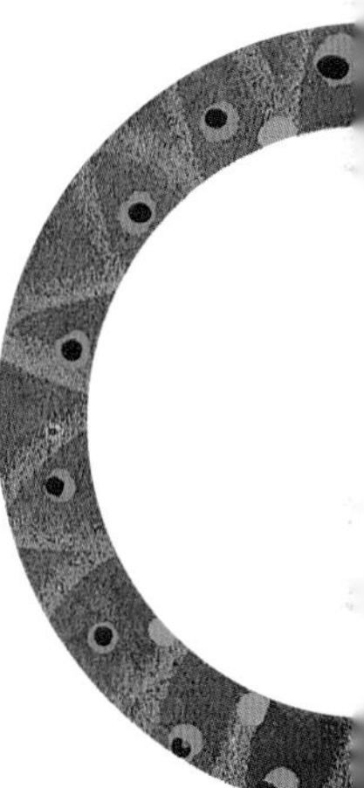

If the will is strong enough, great things can be accomplished; if the will is weak, very little. In every endeavor, it is the man or woman with a firm will who excels.

EKNATH EASWARAN 1910 – 1999

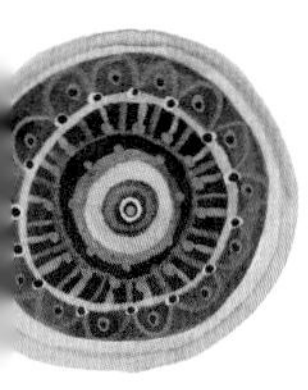
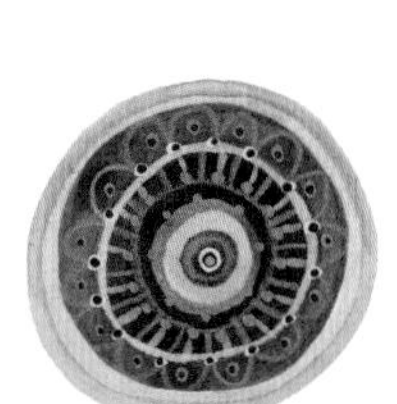
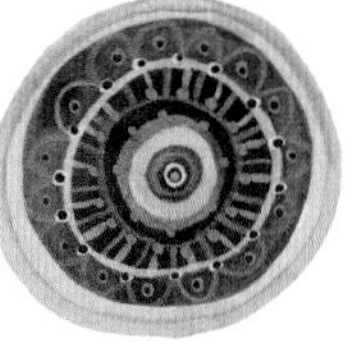
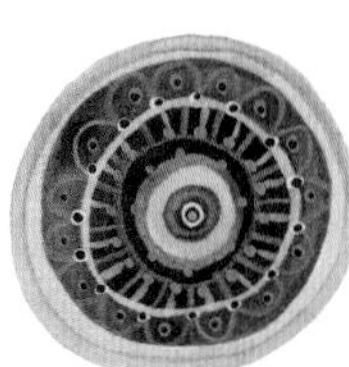
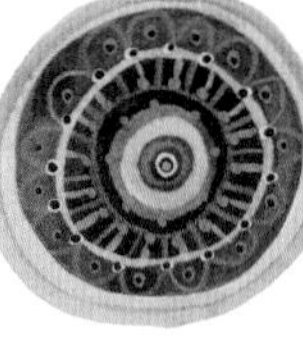

The only thing between you winning or not is this up here and you not believing in yourself.

SALLY GUNNELL, B. 1966

SEPTEMBER 13

As long as you believe in yourself
you can achieve anything.

DAME KELLY HOLMES, B. 1970

No pessimist ever discovered the secrets of the stars,
or sailed to an uncharted land,
or opened a new heaven to the human spirit.

HELEN KELLER 1880 – 1968

Success isn't about walking away.
It is about fixing things.

TOMMY FORD

If you try to do something
or try to go somewhere,
it seldom happens.
However, if you replace 'try' with 'do',
you'll quickly find
that you're far more productive.

ROSEMARY DELANEY

Those that say nothing is impossible in life haven't really thought this through. Plenty of things are impossible. The true gift is to grasp what it is you really want to make possible in your life and then set about making it so.

DR. DALTON EXLEY

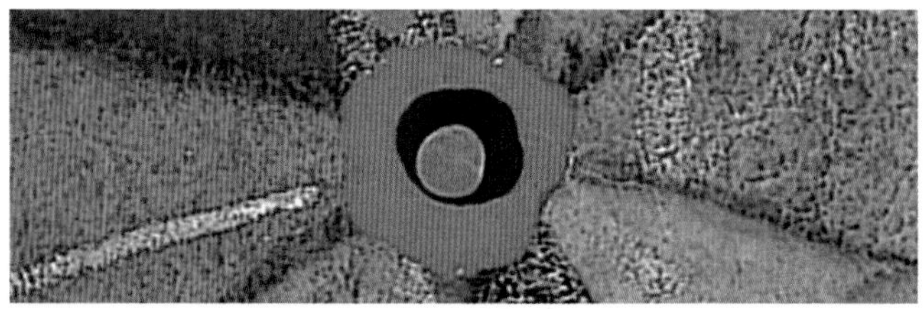

APRIL 24

But now all I need in order to have a future, is to design a future I can manage to get inside of.

FRANCINE JULIAN CLARK

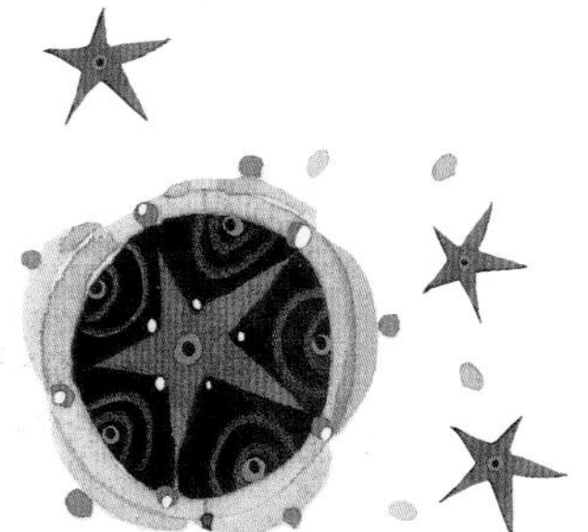

Every time you come to a crossroads ask yourself, "Will I wake up in ten years and regret not taking this path?" That is the path to take.

TAMARA CONNIFF

If you've got a good idea, do something about it.

MICHAEL DELL, B. 1965

It frustrates me to see people waste their lives dreaming of changing something but never getting on and doing it because they (mistakenly) believe they're just not sufficiently talented or capable of achieving anything, feeling there are too many barriers in the way. My attitude is "just go for it!" Even if it doesn't work out, or it takes longer than you thought or is much harder than you thought – at least you've given it a shot.

DAME KELLY HOLMES, B. 1970

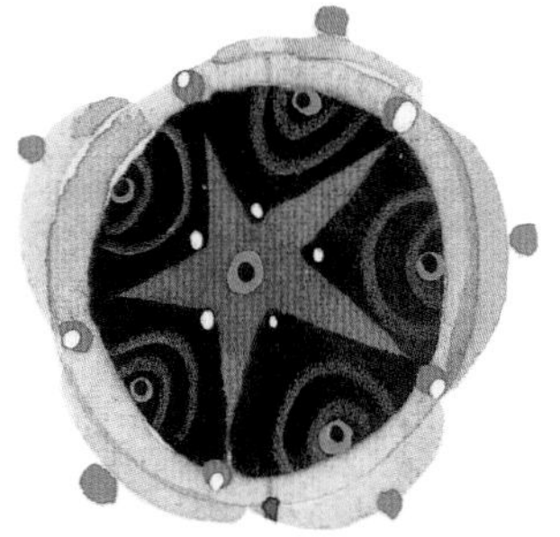

It takes a huge amount of courage and lots of guts to put your dreams in the open, on the line, and say, "Can I really do this or not?" You'll never find out if you don't try.

DR. DALTON EXLEY

The people who succeed best in life are those who take the risk of standing by their own convictions.

JAMES A. GARFIELD 1831 – 1881

Let small, bad things happen so that you can accomplish the huge, positive things.

TIMOTHY FERRISS

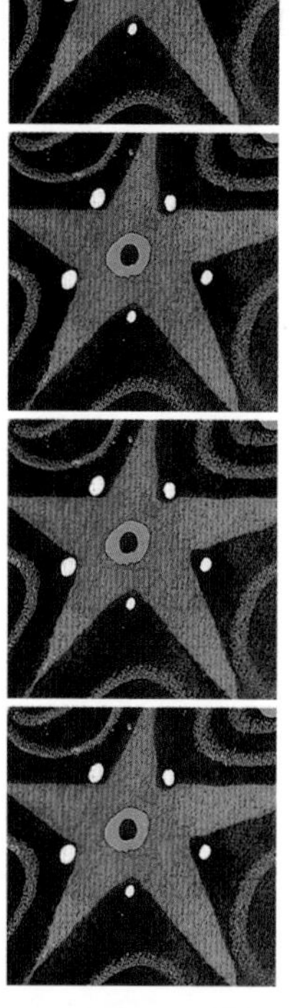

The trick is in what one emphasizes.
We either make ourselves miserable,
or we make ourselves happy.
The amount of work is the same.

CARLOS CASTANEDA

Ever tried. Ever failed. No matter.
Try again. Fail again. Fail better.

SAMUEL BECKETT 1906 – 1989

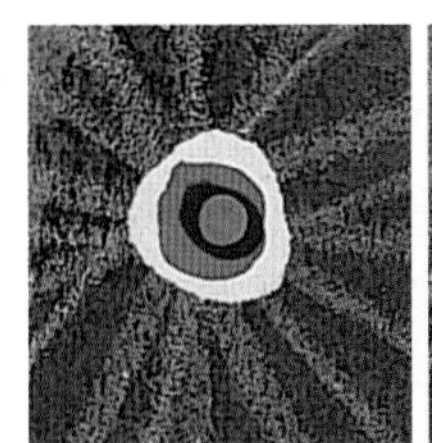

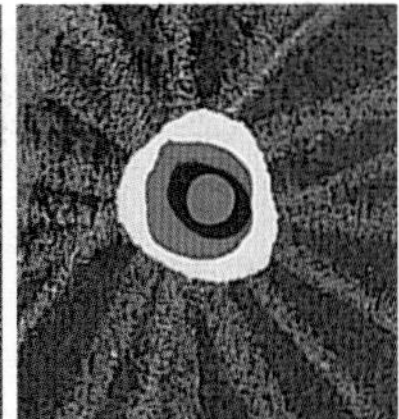

To succeed in this world,
remember these three maxims:
to see is to know; to desire is to be able to;
to dare is to have.

ALFRED DE MUSSET 1810 – 1857

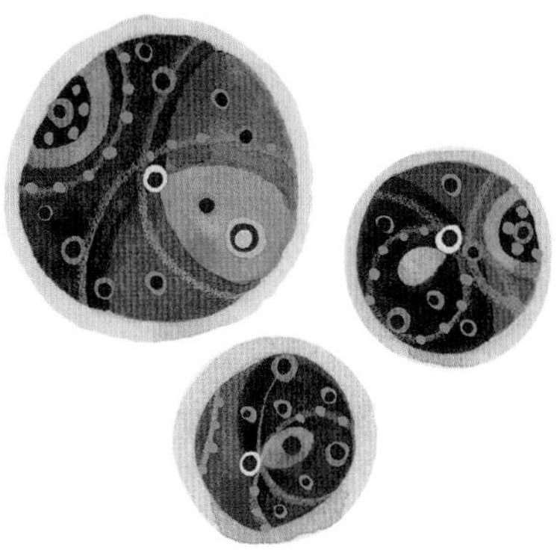

If you aren't willing to fail, you'll never succeed.

MARY KAY ASH 1915 – 2001

It doesn't matter what you mean to do, or what you thought you might do, what matters to the world and the people in it is what you actually do.

FROM "THE FRIENDSHIP BOOK OF FRANCIS GAY"

It is better to wear out than rust out.

RICHARD CUMBERLAND 1732 – 1811

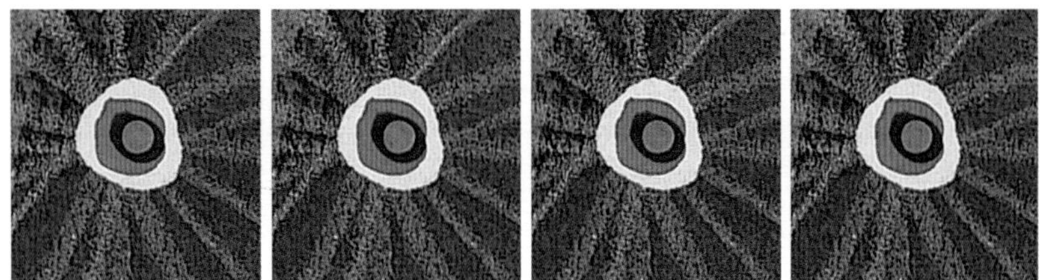

Don't be worried about failing,
be a glorious enthusiastic failure
rather than a tired and timid
traveller on a trouble-free road.

DR. GEORGE CAREY, B. 1935

Do not suppose opportunity will knock twice at your door.

SEBASTIEN CHAMFORT 1741 – 1794

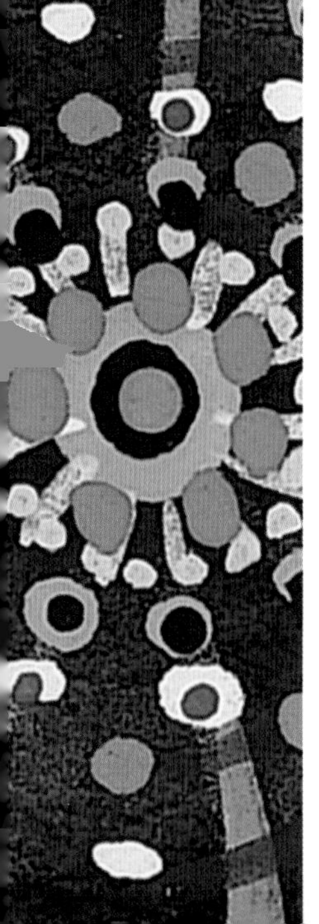

We should never give up on our hopes and dreams. The path may be rocky and twisted, but the world is waiting for that special contribution each of us was born to make.

MARILYN JOHNSON KONDWANI

If you're doing what you believe you should be doing then don't ever stop. Persevere, carry on, get round the obstacles. Get to where you want to go, be what you want to be.

DR. DALTON EXLEY

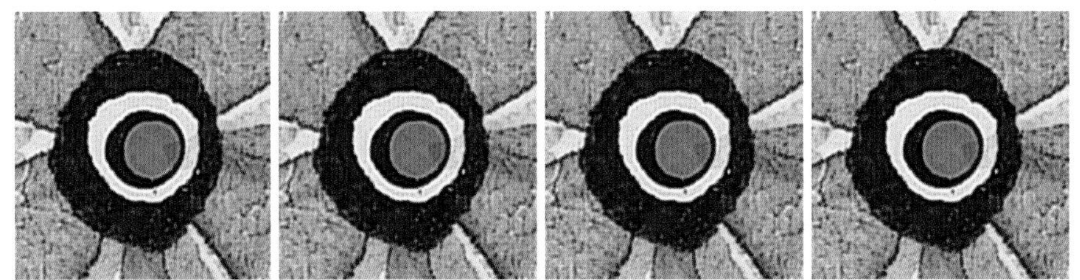

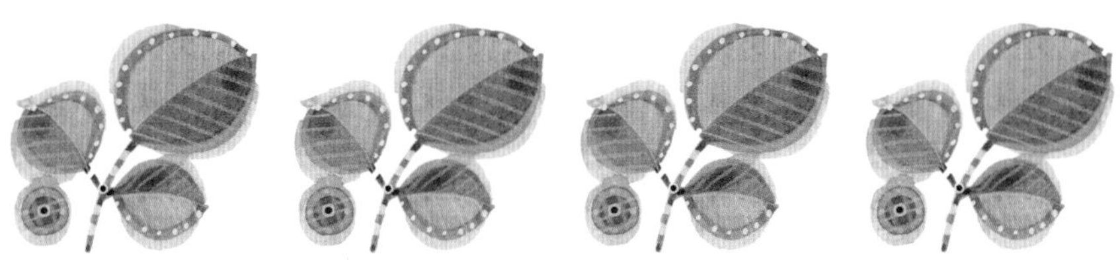

If you're open to the world around you, you'll get the most out of it and eventually you'll get to where you want to be.

ROSEMARY DELANEY

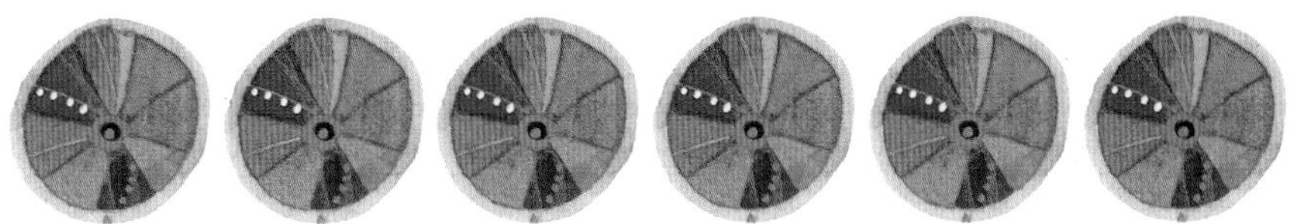

You find that you have peace of mind and can enjoy yourself, get more sleep, and rest when you know that it was a hundred percent effort that you gave – win or lose.

GORDIE HOWE

Between saying and doing,
many a pair of shoes is worn out.

ITALIAN PROVERB

When inspiration does not come to me,
I go halfway to meet it.

SIGMUND FREUD 1856 – 1939

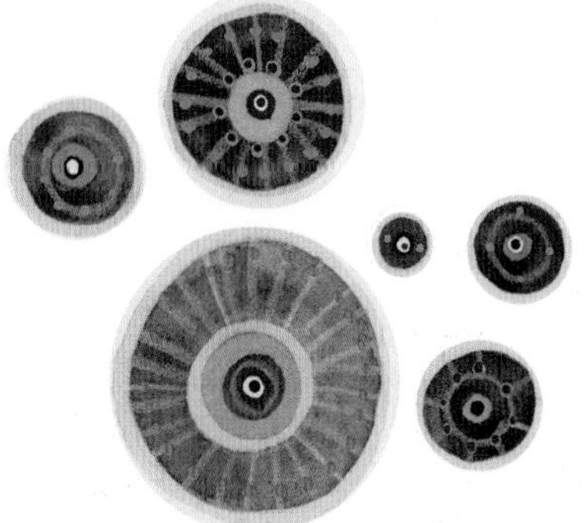

If you have an idea, whatever age you are,
if you have the right ingredients it will be a success,
you just have to go for it and see what happens.
Don't be shy; anyone can make a difference.

ANGELA BAKER

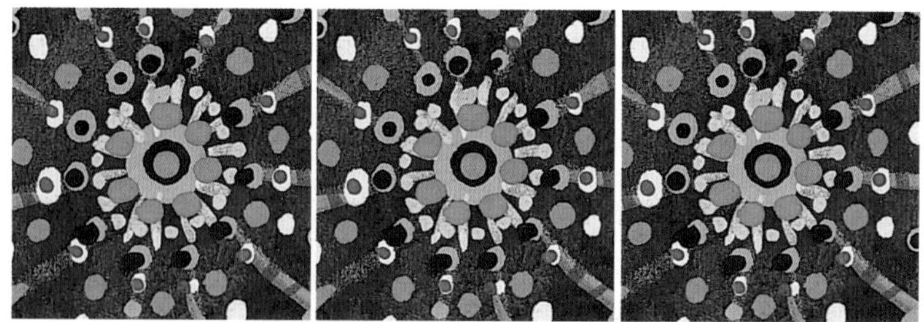

We are creators, and we can form today the world we personally shall be living in tomorrow.

ROBERT COLLIER 1885 – 1950

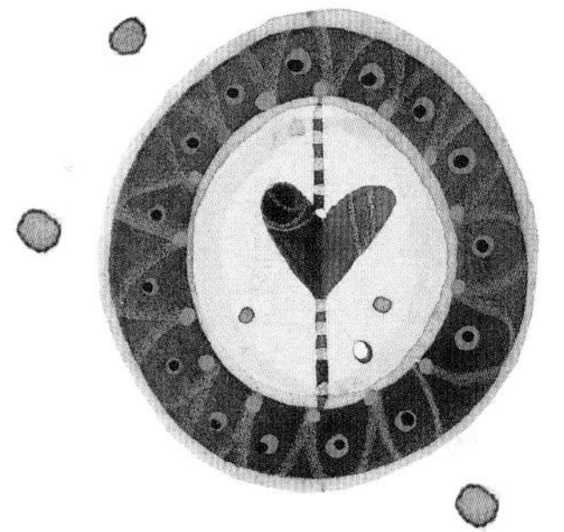

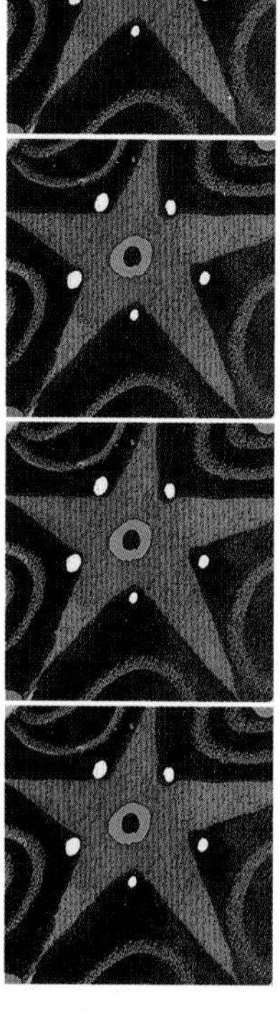

Feel the fear, and do it anyway.

SUSAN JEFFERS

You must accept that you might fail; then, if you do your best and still don't win, at least you can be satisfied that you've tried. If you don't accept failure as a possibility, you don't set high goals, you don't branch out, you don't try – you don't take the risk.

ROSALYNN CARTER, B. 1927

Obstacles in the pathway of
the weak become stepping stones
in the pathway of the strong.

THOMAS CARLYLE 1795 – 1881

It's great to be praised, congratulated and told you're such a success, but it's better and much more ultimately satisfying to know deep down that you've done the best you could. That's real achievement, that's true success.

DR. DALTON EXLEY

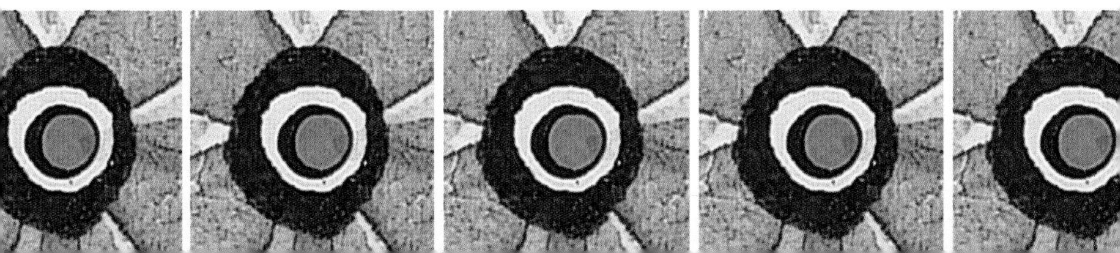

Success is often achieved by those who don't know that failure is inevitable.

COCO CHANEL 1883 – 1971

The world makes way for the person who knows where they are going.

RALPH WALDO EMERSON 1803 – 1882

The only people
who never fail are those
who never try.

ILKA CHASE 1900 – 1978

There is nothing like a dream to create the future.

VICTOR HUGO 1802 – 1885

Challenges keep life going. If you don't have a challenge, I think you die. I need challenges. I love challenges.

ELAYNE JONES

Life isn't worth living without taking a few risks.
And sometimes people need a little prodding.
If you're lucky, they'll thank you.

HEATHER HARPHAM KOPP

...I think what's important
is to override one's natural
self-consciousness and embrace
the absolute right to fail;
not to be afraid to take on
huge challenges.

CATE BLANCHETT, B. 1969

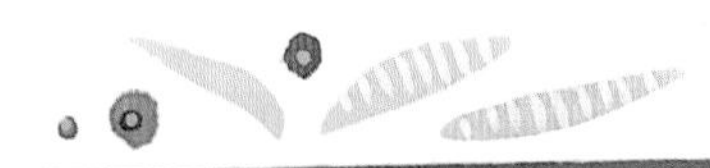

Failure is not trying.
If you never try anything, you'll never succeed.

SHIRLEY CONRAN, B. 1932

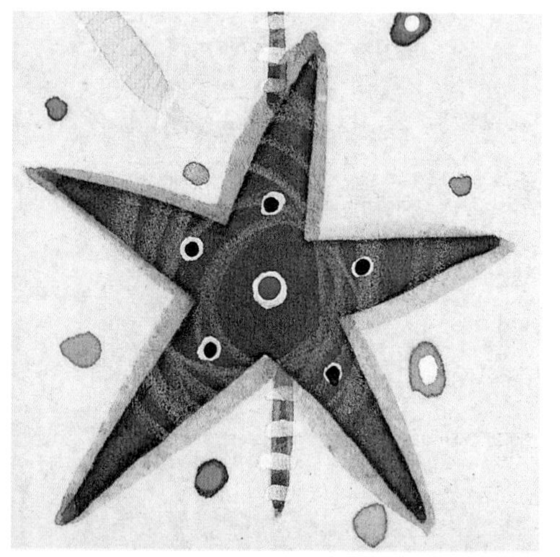

Life isn't fair
and you can moan
about it or you can do
something about it.

ROSEMARY DELANEY

Aim high – there is little virtue in easy victory.

SIR EDMUND HILLARY 1919 – 2008

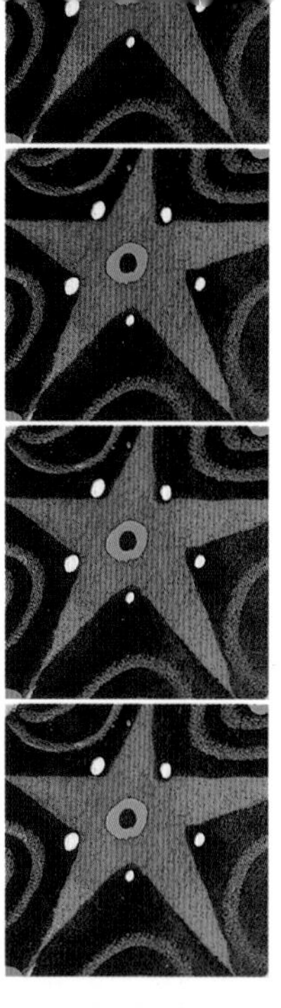

AUGUST 23

Wrestling with your mind weakens you.
When negative thoughts grab hold of you,
observe them without judgment
and they will loosen their grip.

DADI JANKI, B. 1916

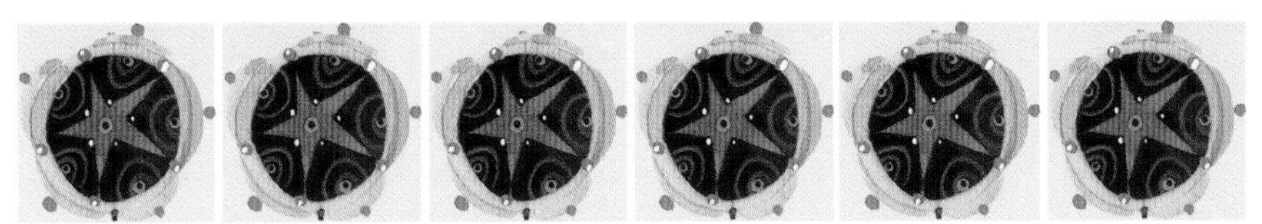

The world's full of great ideas.
Add passion, focus, energy, drive and commitment
to yours or it'll remain just another
of the world's great ideas.

DR. DALTON EXLEY

…there is an enormous pay-off in terms of taking risks, standing up in the world, and facing it with courage. And the pay-off is self-esteem.

JUDY CHICAGO, B. 1939

I never see what has been done, only what remains to be done.

MARIE CURIE 1867 – 1934

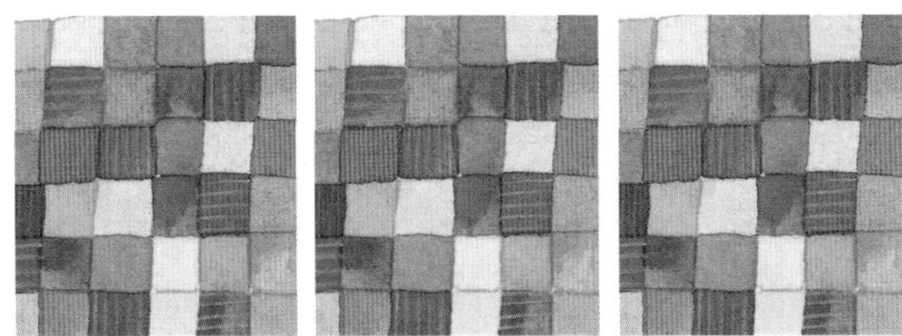

I really believe that if you want to do something enough, then you should do it. Because if you don't, you will regret it.

PHILIP HUGHES, B. 1959

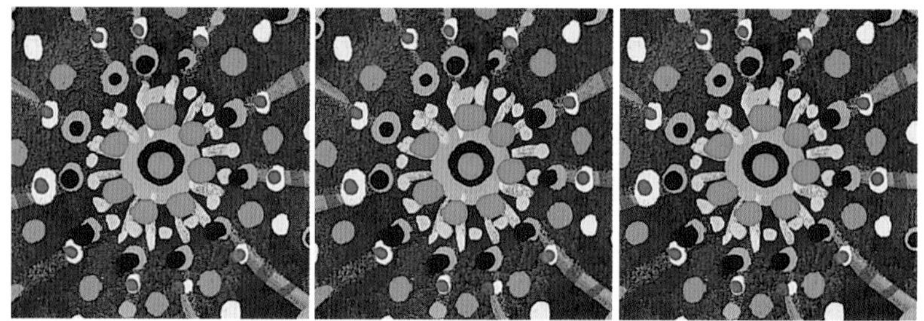

It is never too late to be what you might have been.

GEORGE ELIOT (MARY ANN EVANS) 1819 – 1880

The way to get started
is to quit talking
and begin doing.

WALT DISNEY 1901 – 1966

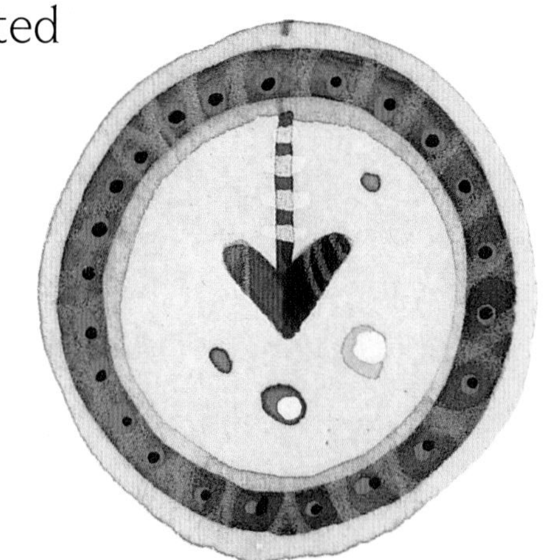

Those who are lifting the world upward and onward are those who encourage more than criticize.

ELIZABETH HARRISON

AUGUST 19

Have confidence in yourself to do
what you think is right.
Fear not what others might say.
Press ahead with determination and dignity.
Strive with all the energy you have.
Ignore criticism.
Have the strength to pursue your vision.
And in the end you will achieve your goal.

DEREK DOBSON

Without risk you can't experience life. There have to be risks, physically and mentally, taken by everyone.

BEN FOGLE, B. 1973

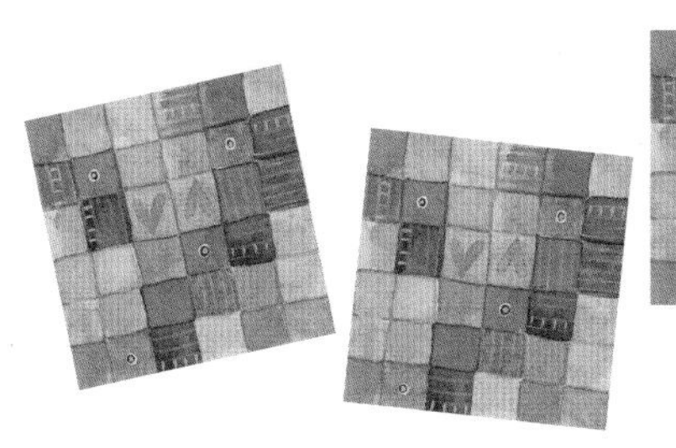
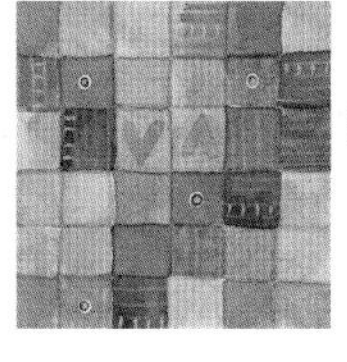
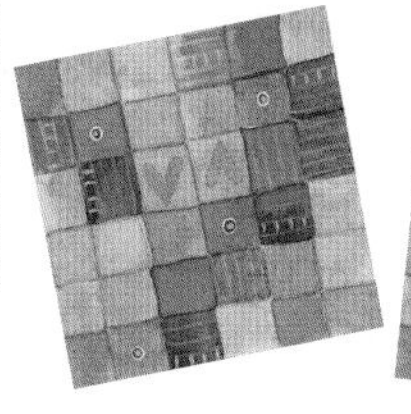
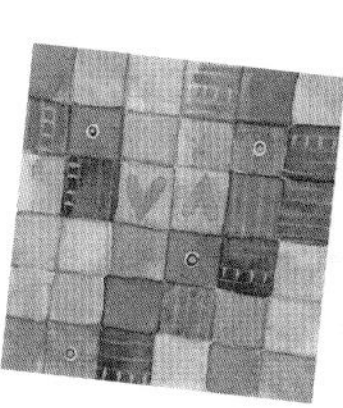

If You Think You Can Or You Can't – You're Right.

HENRY FORD 1863 – 1947

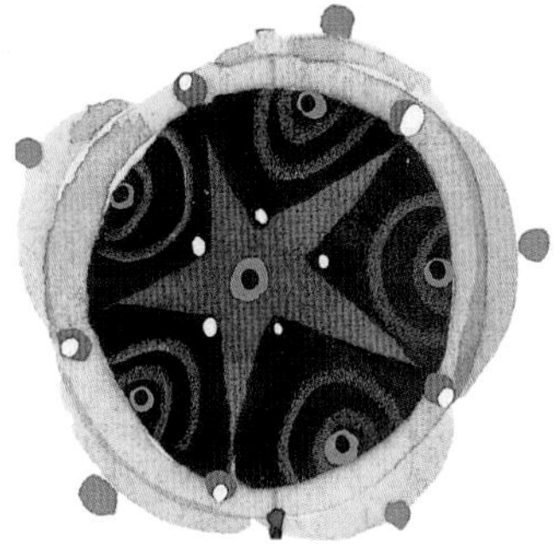

A somebody was once a nobody who wanted to and did.

JOHN BURROUGHS 1837 – 1921

A rock pile ceases to be a rock pile the moment a single man contemplates it, bearing within him the image of a cathedral.

ANTOINE DE SAINT-EXUPERY 1900 – 1944

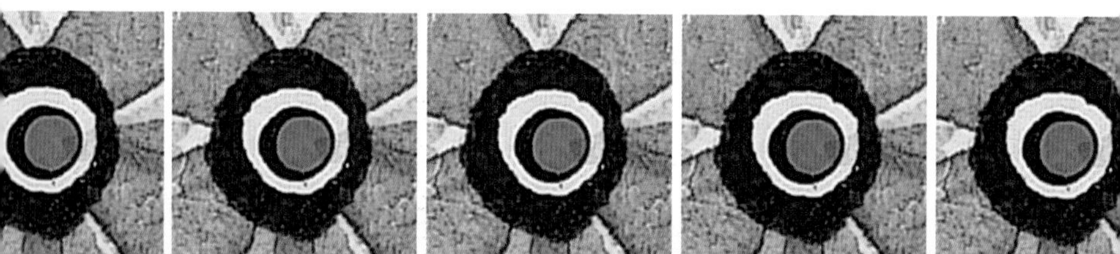

Stickability, stickability, stickability. If you want something really, really badly, then be persistent, focus and strive towards your goal. You'll get there.

DR. DALTON EXLEY

Come to the edge, Life said.
They said: We are afraid.
Come to the edge, Life said.
They came. It pushed Them....
And They flew.

GUILLAUME APOLLINAIRE 1880 – 1918

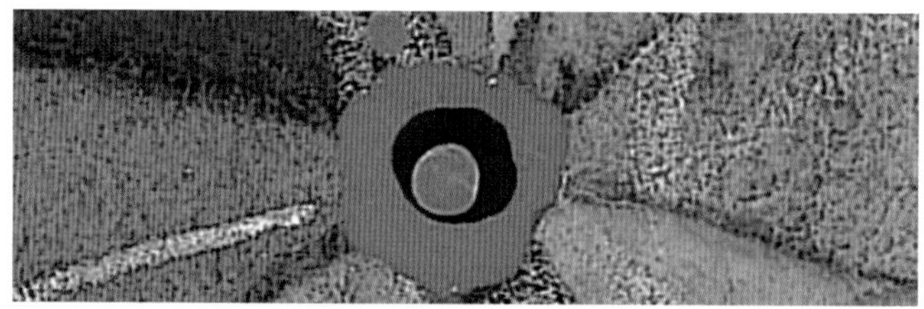

Basically, you have two options in this world – live, or die. And if you're going to live life crippled by fears of your own failings, or of your eventual and inevitable death, then tell me what exactly is the point?

DEBBIE HARRY, B. 1945

Every day must come to you as a new hope, a new promise, a new aspiration. If you think that tomorrow will be just another day like all the days you have already seen, you will make no progress. Every day you have to energize yourself anew. For it is only with newness that you can succeed and transcend yourself.

SRI CHINMOY 1931 – 2007

You have to create your own opportunities,
I think that's what today is all about...
You have to take the plunge to do things,
become more daring, not necessarily play safe
or copy others. It is being you.

EVELYN GLENNIE, B. 1965

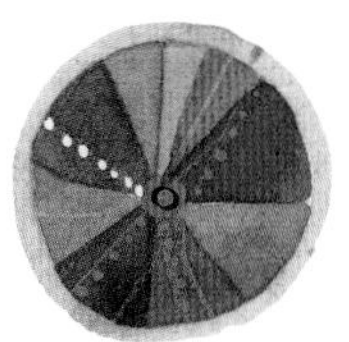
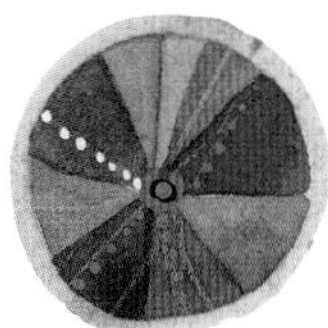
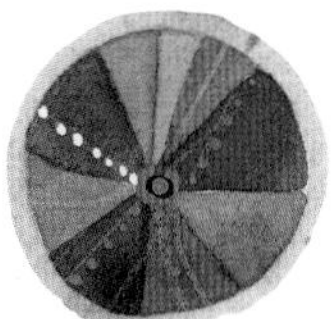
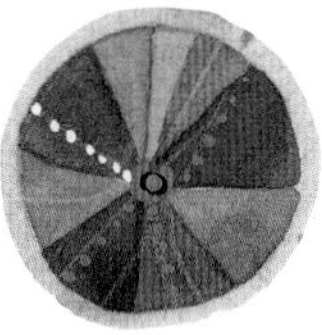

Accept that all of us can be hurt,
that all of us can – and surely will
at times – fail. Other vulnerabilities,
like being embarrassed or risking love,
can be terrifying too. I think we should
follow a simple rule:
if we can take the worst, take the risk.

DR. JOYCE BROTHERS 1927 – 2013

Think about that next time you say to yourself, "I can't." Try to get to the bottom of your self-doubt. Why are you really saying "I can't?" Does it just seem too hard? Or perhaps it might not come to you as quickly as you'd like? Remember, if you want something enough and are prepared to give 100 per cent to achieve it, then you can. You just have to believe you can, and keep reminding yourself that you can, and be patient.

DAME KELLY HOLMES, B. 1970

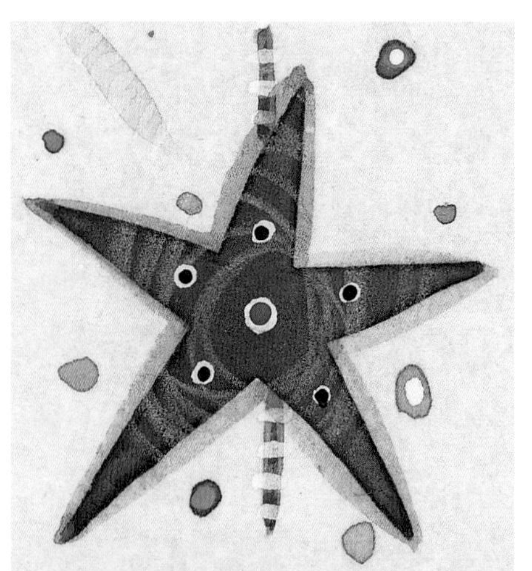

Either you decide to stay in the shallow end of the pool or you go out in the ocean.

CHRISTOPHER REEVE
1952 – 2004

I believe that life should be lived
so vividly and so intensely
that thoughts of another life,
or of a longer life, are not necessary.

MARJORY STONEMAN DOUGLAS 1890 – 1998

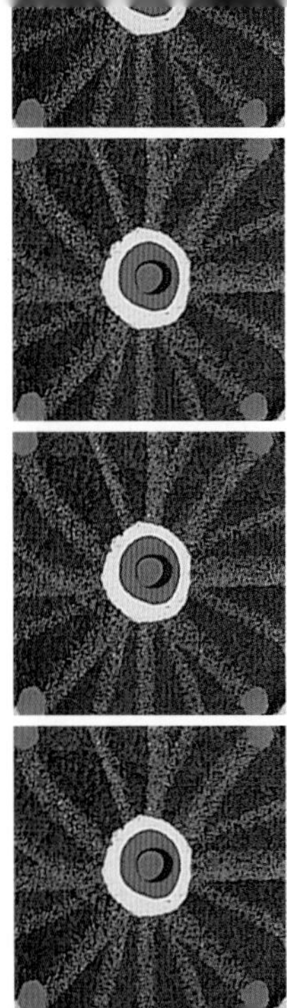

AUGUST 12

What exhausts a person is not hard work, but the strain of feeling compartmentalized, limited, cut off, boxed in.

FRANCES HESSELBEIN

MAY 24

Press on! A better fate awaits you.

VICTOR HUGO 1802 – 1885

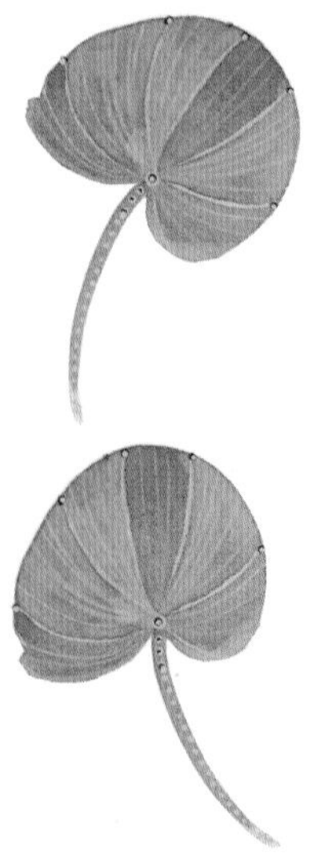

What lies behind us,
and what lies before us
are tiny matters,
compared to what lies
within us.

RALPH WALDO EMERSON 1803 – 1882

Having a purpose, goals to reach for and attain, makes life worth living. There's nothing worse than a purposeless existence, so be brave, and move onwards, with a smile on your face and a happy heart.

DR. DALTON EXLEY

Our lives improve only when we take chances – and the first and most difficult risk we can take is to be honest with ourselves.

WALTER ANDERSON, B. 1916

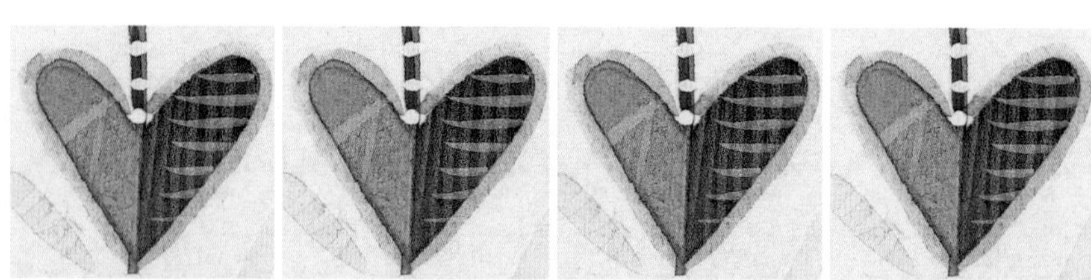

There is a vitality, a life force, an energy,
a quickening that is translated through you
into action and because there is only
one of you in all time, this expression
is unique. And if you block it,
it will never exist through any other medium
and be lost, the world will not have it.

MARTHA GRAHAM 1894 – 1991

The thing you have got to learn is that nobody gives you power. You just take it.

ROSEANNE BARR, B. 1952

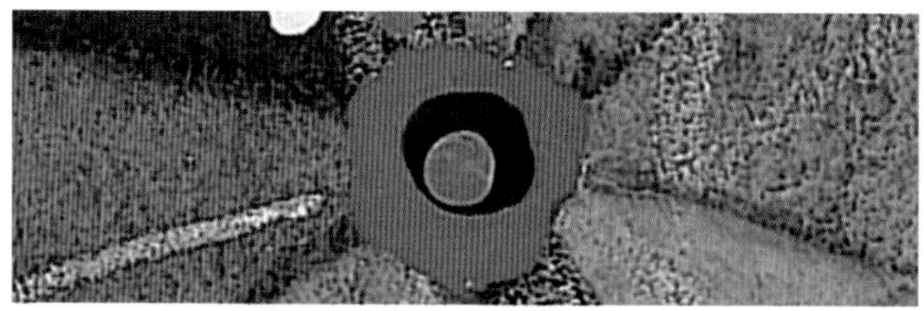

Destiny is not a matter of chance,
it is a matter of choice.

WILLIAM JENNINGS BRYAN 1860 – 1925

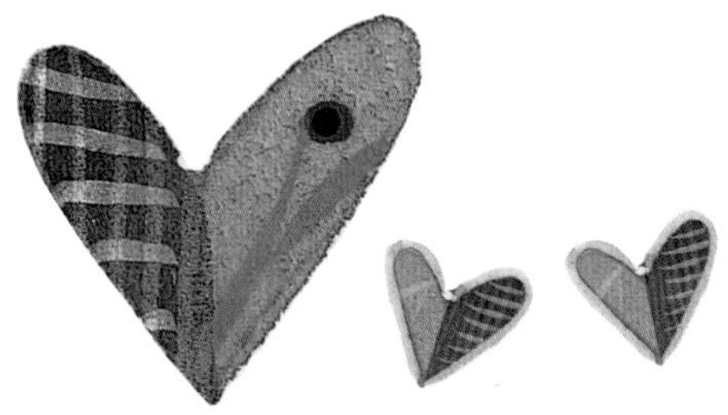

OBSTACLES ARE THOSE FRIGHTFUL THINGS YOU SEE WHEN YOU TAKE YOUR EYES OFF YOUR GOAL.

HENRY FORD 1863 – 1947

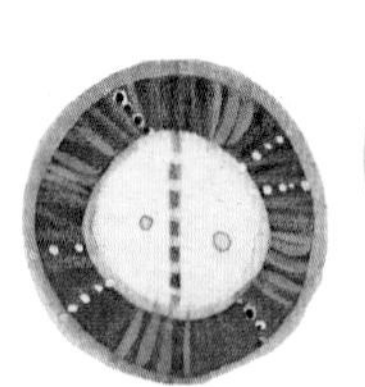
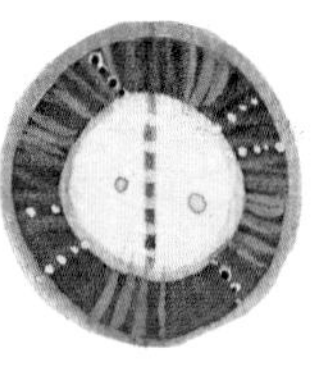
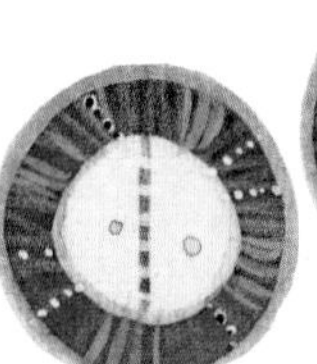
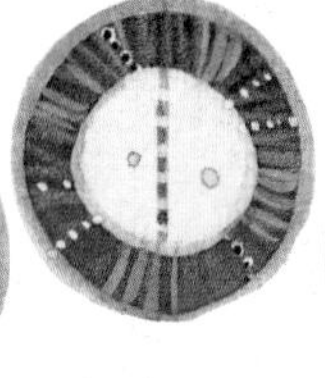
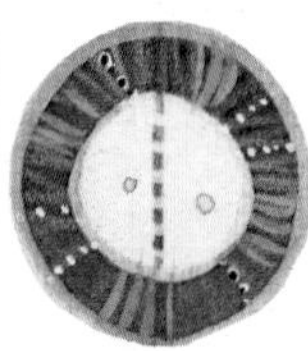

MAY 28

Life is a do-it-yourself kit.

PHYLLIS DILLER 1917 – 2012

The best thing you can do is believe in yourself. Don't be afraid to try. Don't be afraid to fail. Just try again.

JUDY GREEN HERBSTREIT

The boldest and most ridiculous
hope has sometimes been
the cause of extraordinary success.

LUC DE VAUVENARGUES

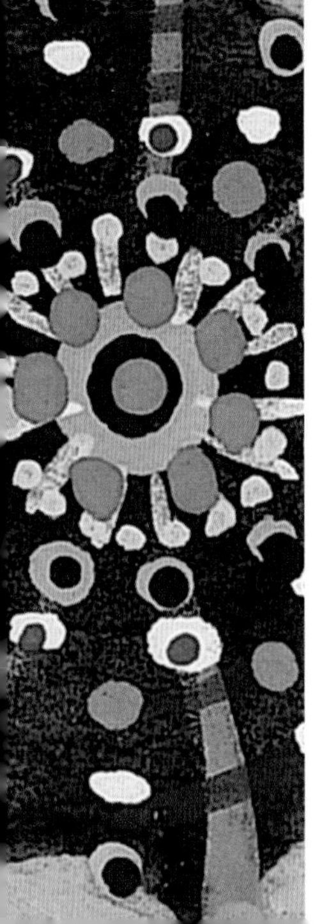

When you want to succeed in life and achieve your objectives you have to take risks. Sometimes you'll fail and that's part of learning to succeed. But sometimes you can turn a losing situation into a win by having the determination, the courage, the fighting spirit to make it happen, to win.

BILL CULLEN, B. 1942

There are no mistakes, only feedback.

PETER JONES, B. 1966

The person who makes
a success of living is
the one who sees his goal
steadily and aims for
it unswervingly.
That is dedication.

CECIL B. DE MILLE 1881 – 1959

Seeds of greatness within!
If you think you have it, grab it and run with it!

DR. DALTON EXLEY

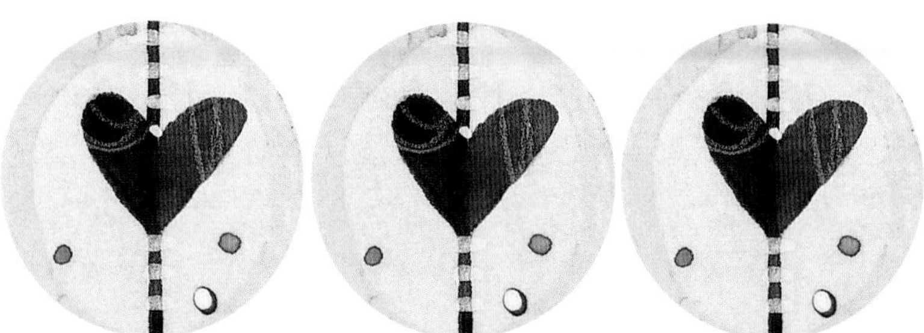

You have your brush, you have your colours, you paint paradise, then in you go.

NIKOS KAZANTZAKIS 1883 – 1957

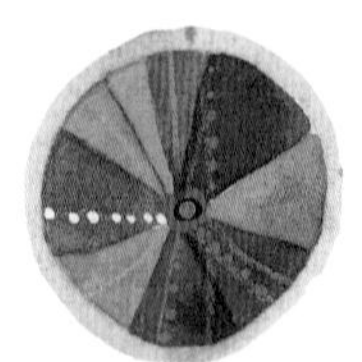
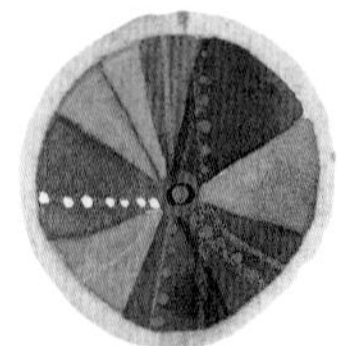
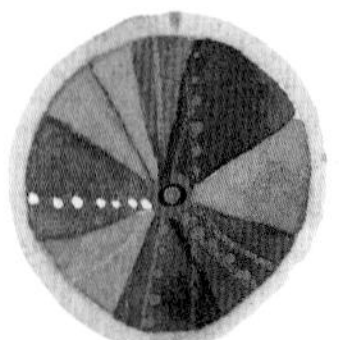
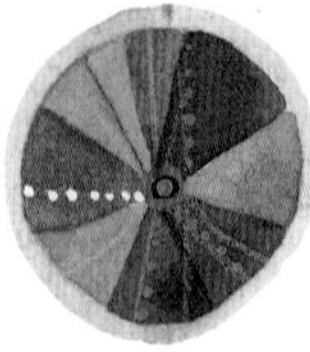

There's a way to do it better – find it.

THOMAS EDISON 1847 – 1931

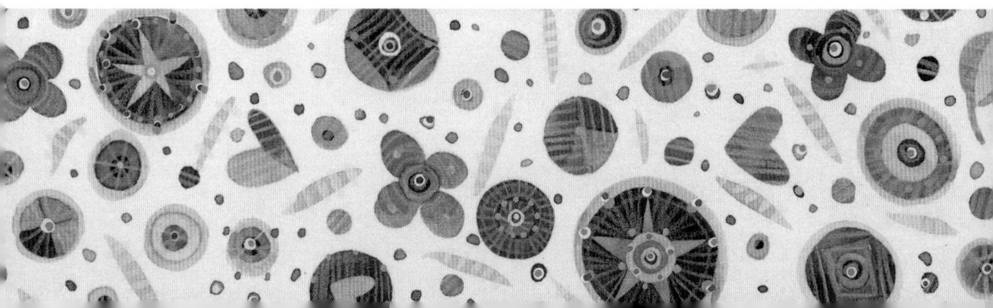

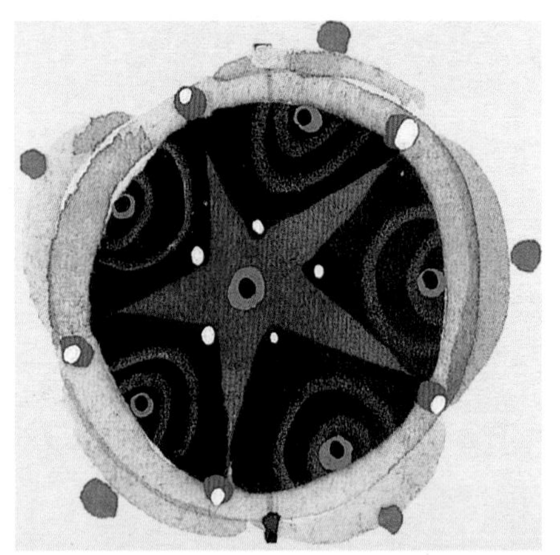

To dare is to live.

SUZANNE C. COLE

JUNE 2

Live your life while you have it.
Life is a splendid gift – there is nothing small about it.

FLORENCE NIGHTINGALE 1820 – 1910

Life's been very good. It has its problems: we have hurricanes, we have storms, and then the sun comes out and it's sunny again. That's the way life is. If we're looking for a smooth ride, it doesn't happen. There will be highs, lows, and plateaus, but we live to have an opportunity to climb every mountain in our path. We have an opportunity to embrace the world, to embrace other people, to love other people.

DR. LORRAINE HALE 1926 – 2013

People for the sake of getting a living forget to live.

MARGARET FULLER 1810 – 1850

I struggle to live for the beauty of a pansy, for a little
black baby's song, for my lover's laugh.
I struggle for the blaze of pink across the evening sky...
I struggle for life and the pursuit of its happiness.
I struggle to fill my house with joy.

STEPHANIE BYRD

A new life begins for us with every second.
Let us go forward joyously to meet it.
We must press on, whether we will or no,
and we shall walk better with our eyes before us
than with them ever cast behind.

JEROME K. JEROME 1859 – 1927

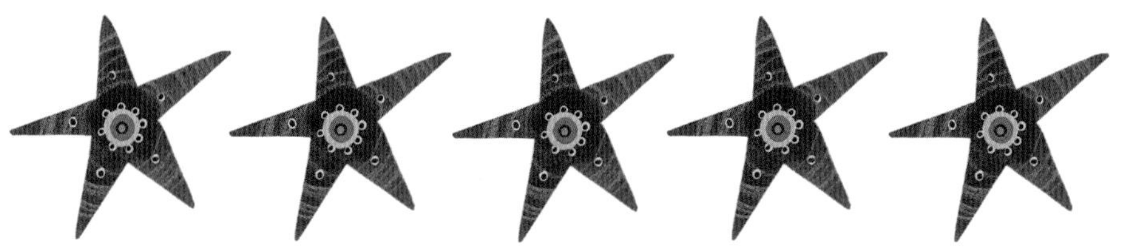

The starting point of all achievement is desire.
Keep this constantly in mind.
Weak desire brings weak results.

NAPOLEON HILL 1883 – 1970

The world you desire can be won,
it exists, it is real, it is possible, it's yours.

AYN RAND 1905 – 1982

Anyone who has never made a mistake has never tried anything new.

ALBERT EINSTEIN 1879 – 1955

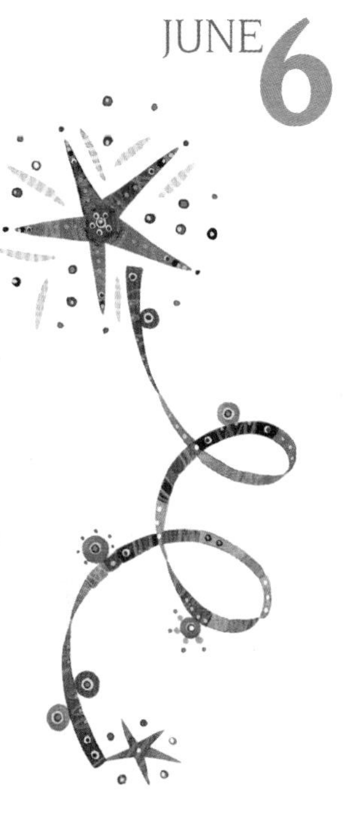

Just as they say, if you fall off a horse
then get straight back up on it;
don't give up or become scared of horses.
The same applies to setbacks towards
your goals. Get straight back and on with
your work. You can fall, we all do at times,
but never, never be defeated. Always
upwards, always onwards.

DR. DALTON EXLEY

If you fail, will you be seriously damaged or merely embarrassed?
If you succeed, will it change your life for the better?
When you can persuade yourself that your dream is worthwhile
and achievable – then say thank you to the doubters
and take the plunge…

GILBERT E. KAPLAN

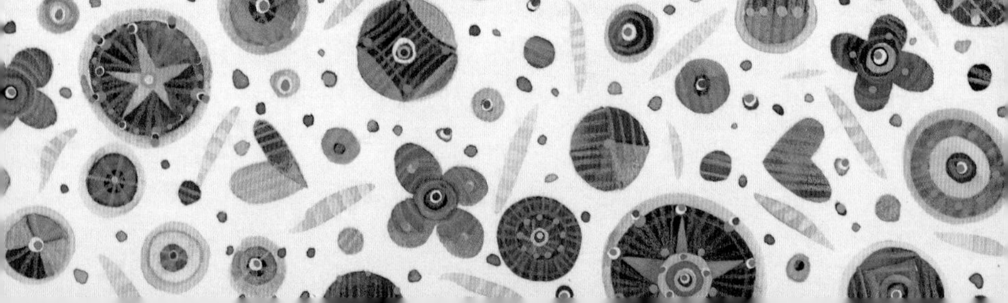

We cannot escape fear. We only transform it into a companion that accompanies us on all our exciting adventures... Take a risk a day – one small or bold stroke that will make you feel great once you have done it.

SUSAN JEFFERS

Life is not easy for any of us, but what of it?
We must have perseverance and confidence in ourselves.
We must believe we are each gifted for something
and that this thing must be attained.

MARIE CURIE 1867 – 1934

JUNE 8

Slow down? Rest? With all eternity before me?

SARAH BERNHARDT 1844 – 1923

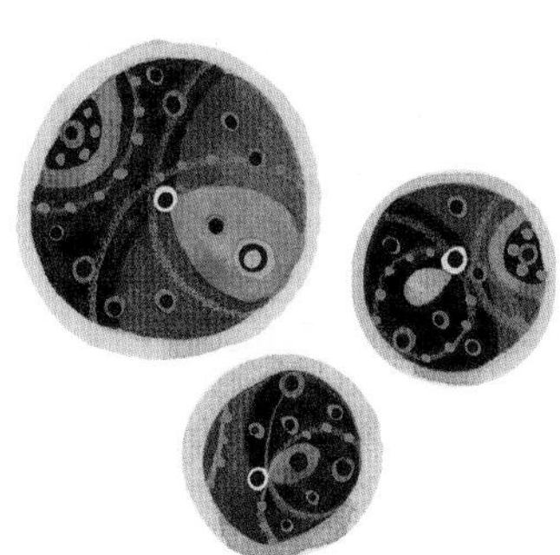

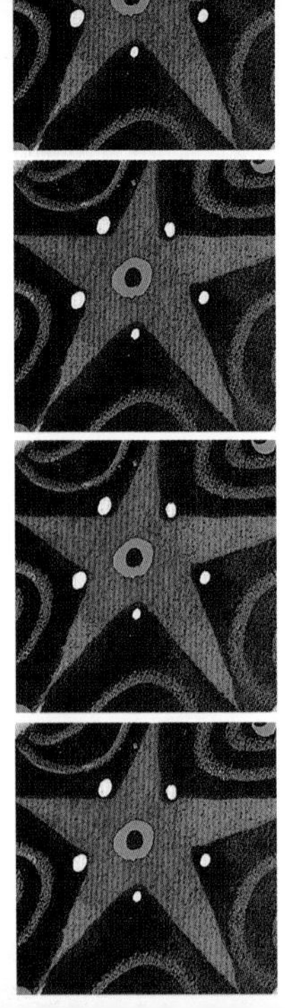

Believe in what you're doing.
If you've got an idea that's really powerful,
you've just got to ignore
the people who tell you it won't work.

MICHAEL DELL, B. 1965

You either shrink and hide or you throw
your shoulders back and charge right in.
I learned that charging felt more comfortable for me.

MINNIE DRIVER, B. 1971

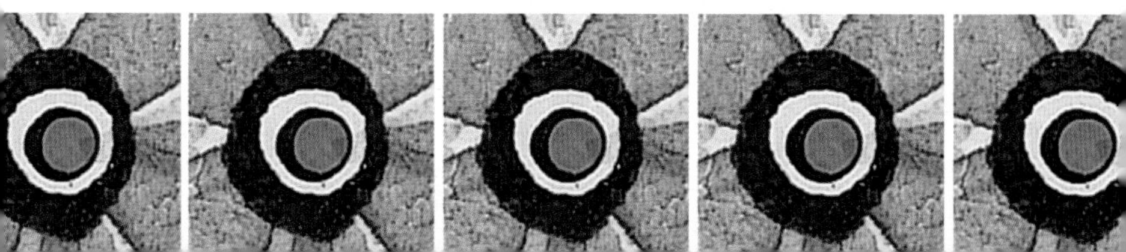

JULY 26

He who deliberates fully before taking the next step will spend his entire life on one leg.

CHINESE PROVERB

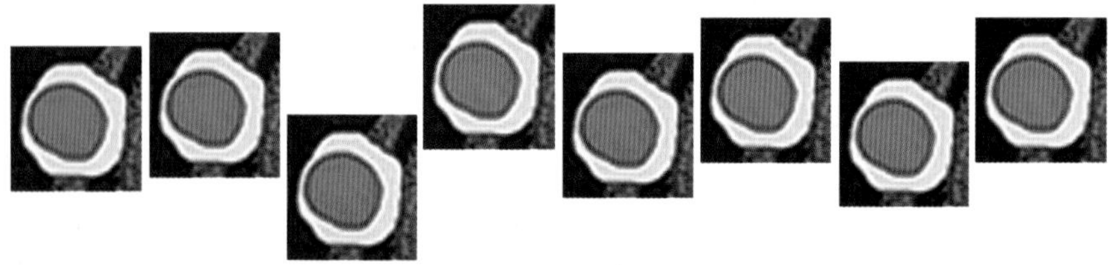

I might have been born in a hovel, but I determined to travel with the wind and the stars.

JACQUELINE COCHRAN 1908 – 1980

JULY 25

[There] is a need to find and sing
our own song, to stretch our limbs
and shake them in a dance so wild
that nothing can roost there,
that stirs the yearning
for solitary voyage.

BARBARA LAZEAR ASCHER

Be true to who you are,
and never give up on your dreams.

JACKIE JOYNER-KERSEE, B. 1962

It's a mistake to put things off because you don't think you'll have long enough to achieve anything. Don't sit around waiting for the "ideal" moment to arrive: make it happen.

DAME KELLY HOLMES, B. 1970

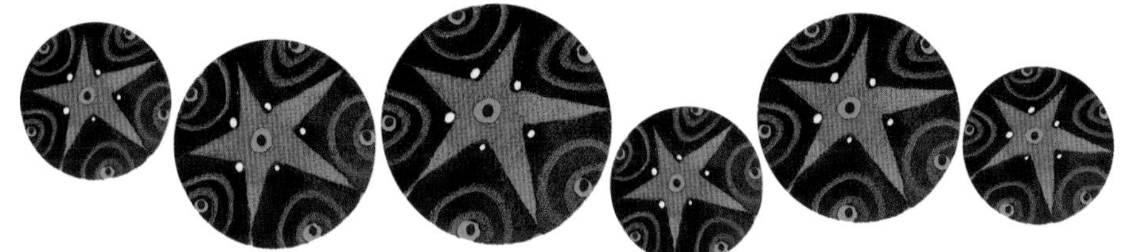

Imagine, near the end of your life, looking back on the dreams and hopes you had. Wouldn't it be so good to think you had done all you could, you had gone for all that mattered, you had lived life to the full and followed your dreams fully. There's always time while your heart still beats.

DR. DALTON EXLEY

Never use the words, "I can't." Say, "I'll try."

RUBY MIDDLETON FORSYTHE

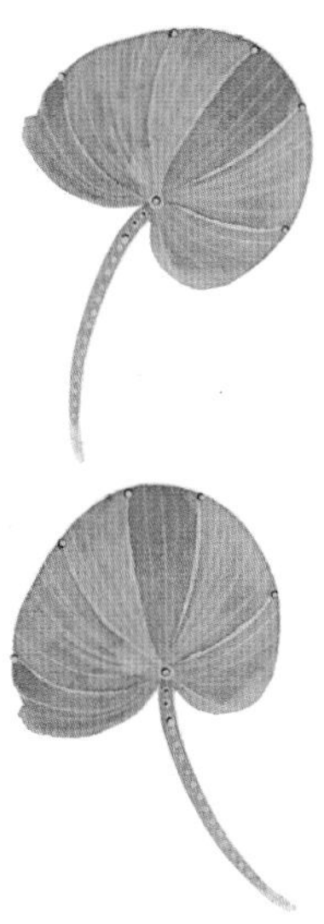

RULE FOR HAPPINESS:
SOMETHING TO DO,
SOMEONE TO LOVE,
SOMETHING TO HOPE FOR.

IMMANUEL KANT 1724 – 1804

To engage in daily combat with yourself
and win, you need a strong project,
strong ambition, and strong passion.
A good means of getting through is defiance,
towards yourself and the world.
"By my own means, away from the tracks you
have made, I will succeed. Never mind
the ambushes and traps, I will succeed."

IRÉNÉE GUILANE DIOH, B. 1948

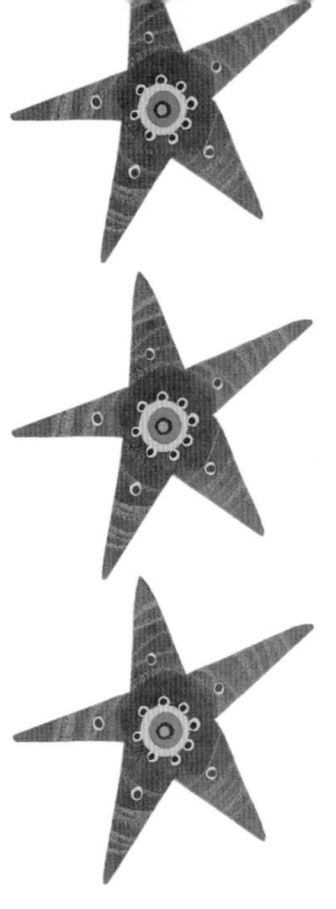

I am only one,
But still I am one.
I cannot do everything,
But still I can do something;
And because I cannot do everything
I will not refuse to do
the something that I can do.

EDWARD EVERETT HALE 1822 – 1909

THE ONLY FAILURE IS NOT TO TRY.

BILL CULLEN, B. 1942

Shout it, play it, love it, all, right now, every time!

ANNIE DILLARD, B. 1945

He who loses wealth loses much;
he who loses a friend loses more;
but he who loses his courage loses all.

MIGUEL DE CERVANTES 1547 – 1616

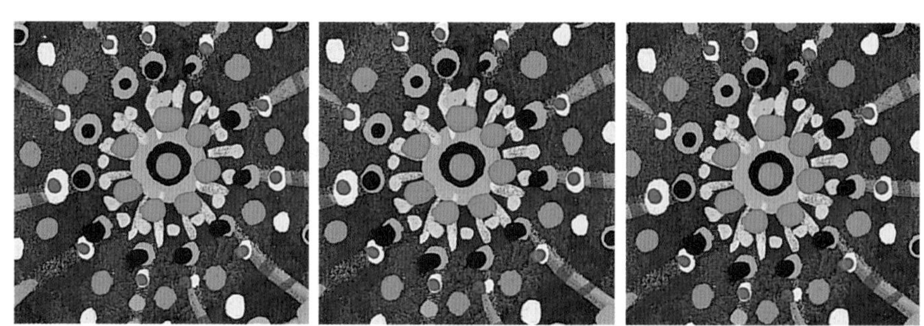

Put a grain of boldness into everything you do.

BALTASAR GRACIAN 1601 – 1658

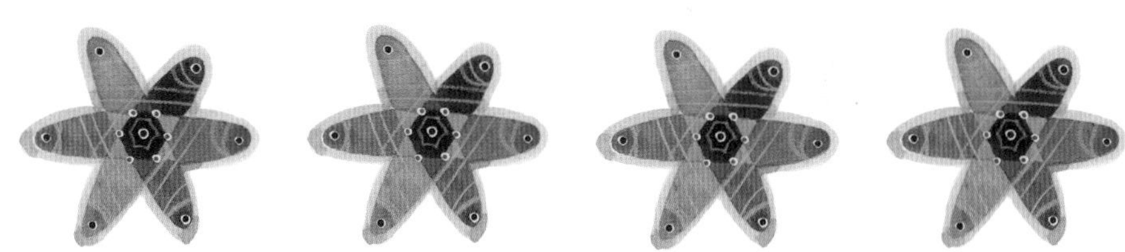

When I started out, people would ask me,
"Who do you think you are?
This is the way things get done."
But if you believe that you have to do things
someone else's way,
you'll never go very far.

PAT HARRISON

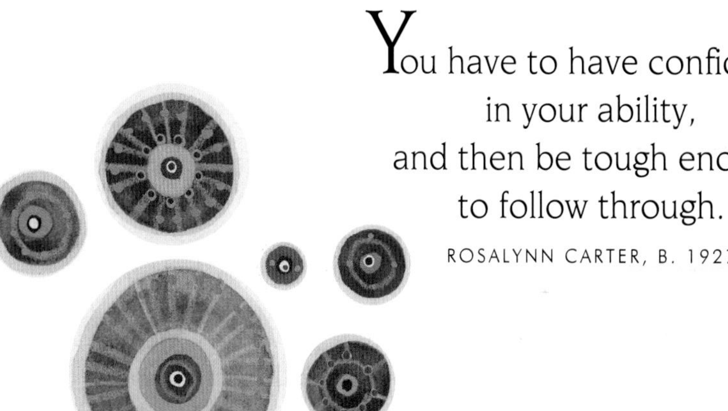

You have to have confidence
in your ability,
and then be tough enough
to follow through.

ROSALYNN CARTER, B. 1927

Courageous risks are life giving, they help you grow, make you brave and better than you think you are.

JOAN L. CURCIO

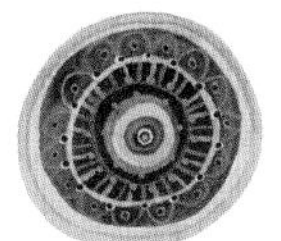 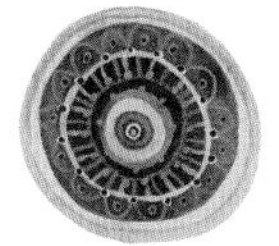 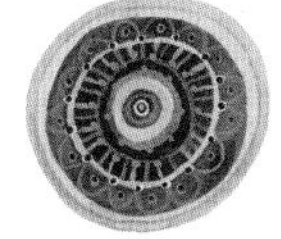 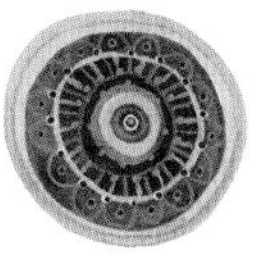 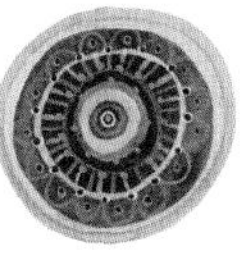 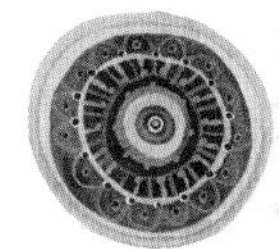

For me it's the things you don't do in life,
rather than the things you do,
that you end up regretting. You only live once,
so live it!

DR. DALTON EXLEY

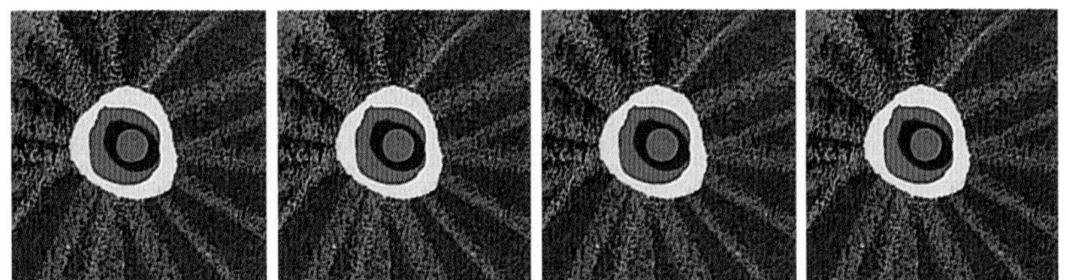

The first step towards success is taken
when you refuse to be a captive of the environment
in which you first find yourself.

MARK CAINE

Your life does not fill a hundred years, but always is it full of a thousand cares. Short the midday, bitter long the nights! Why then do you not grasp the lamp, seeking out for yourself the short lived joys, why not today? Why will you wait year after year?

CHINESE PHILOSOPHER OF THE HAN DYNASTY

...as one goes through life one learns that if you don't paddle your own canoe, you don't move.

KATHARINE HEPBURN 1907 – 2003

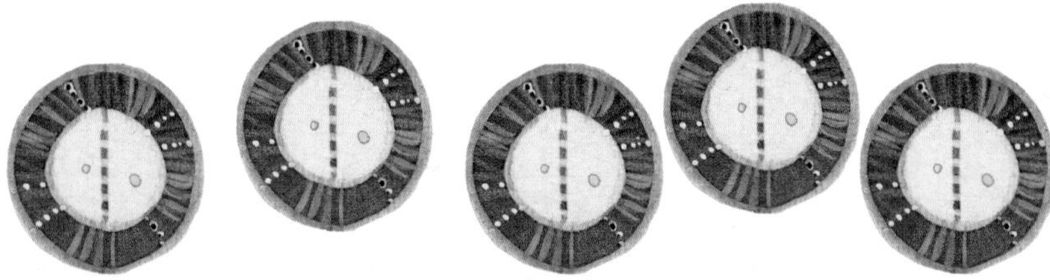

Life is either a daring adventure or nothing. To keep our faces toward change and behave like free spirits in the presence of fate is strength undefeatable.

HELEN KELLER 1880 – 1968

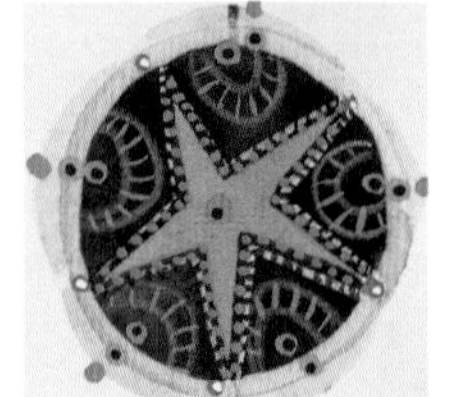

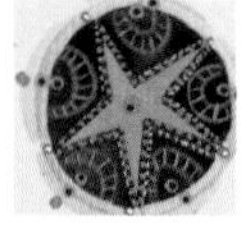

JULY 15

To play it safe is not to play.

ROBERT ALTMAN 1925 – 2006

JUNE 21

When a great adventure is offered, you don't refuse it.

AMELIA EARHART 1898 – 1937

Don't let anyone tell you what you can't do. If you don't succeed, let it be because of you. Don't blame it on other people.

EARVIN "MAGIC" JOHNSON, B. 1959

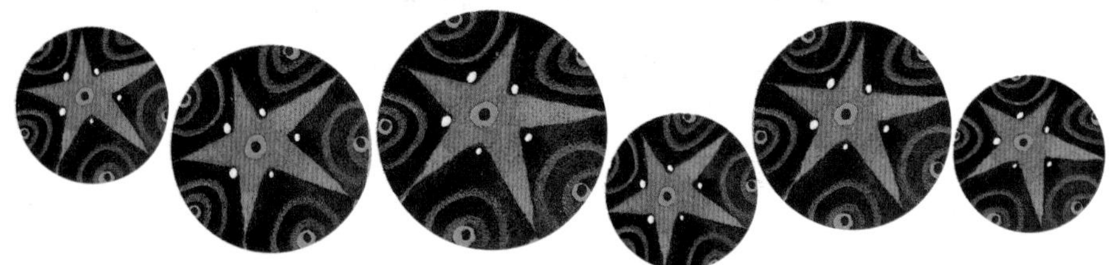

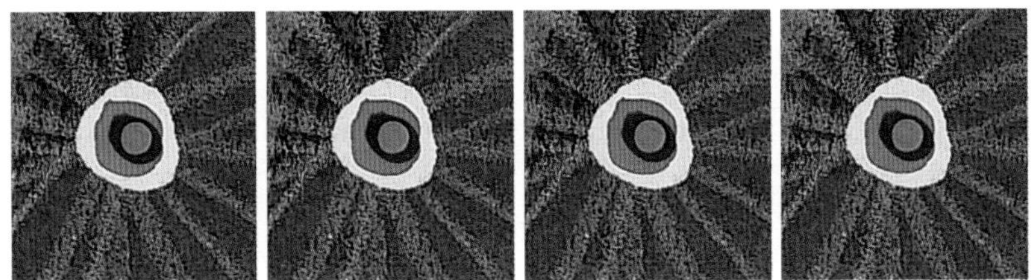

Genius is one per cent inspiration, ninety-nine per cent perspiration.

THOMAS EDISON 1847 – 1931

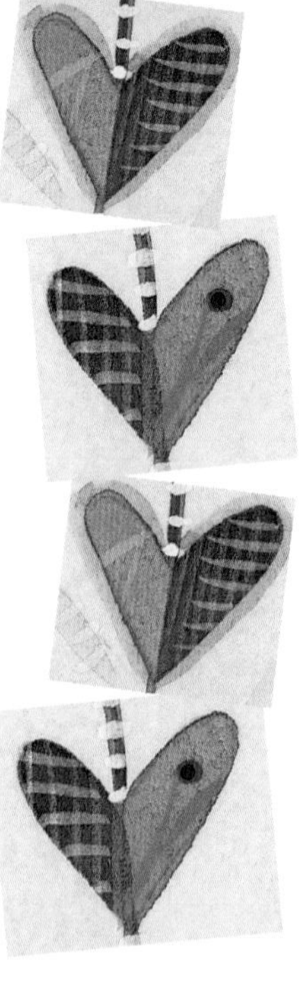

Success always lurks
just beyond your comfort zone.
You can see it;
you can taste it.
You just need to want it enough.

ROSEMARY DELANEY

...if you want something very badly,
you can achieve it. It may take patience,
very hard work, a real struggle, and a long time;
but it can be done.
That much faith is a prerequisite
of any undertaking....

MARGO JONES

It's amazing to see how far hope can take even the lowliest football club, when belief runs high that they really can win something.

DR. DALTON EXLEY

JUNE 24

Successful people often talk about the wealth of experience lying behind their great success. Experience translates here as meaning lots of wrong turns and failures along the way. Don't ever be afraid to fail. It is part of the process of gaining experience. Often it is only by finding out how things have gone wrong that you know how to do them right. Take it all in your stride on the road to success.

DR. DALTON EXLEY

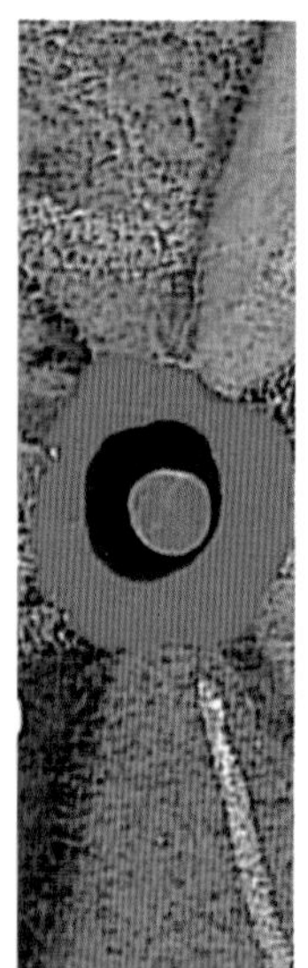

The word "impossible" is black.
"I can" is like a flame of gold.

CATHERINE COOKSON 1906 – 1998

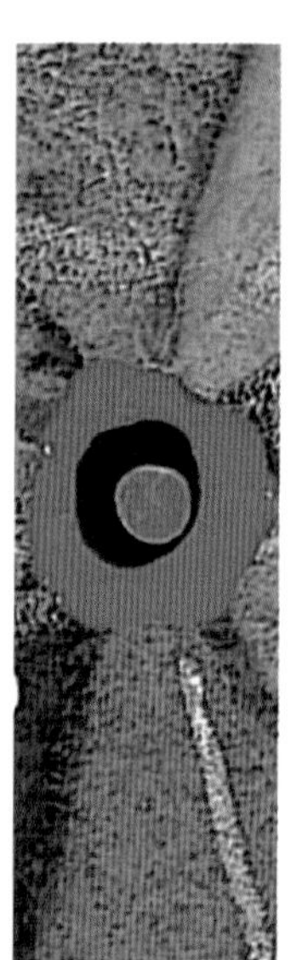

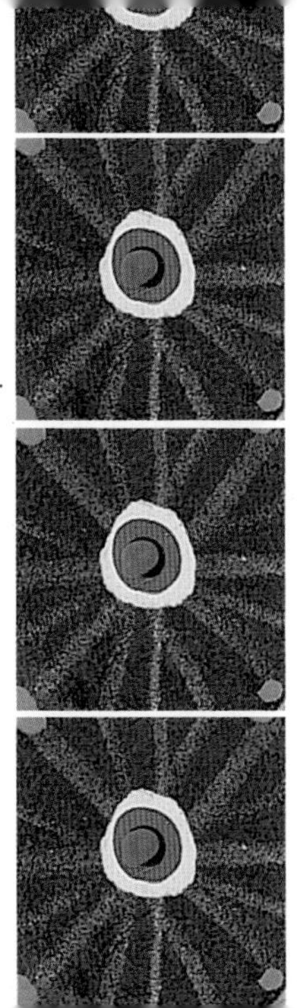

Failure can be one of the best lessons. Fear of failure stops people doing great things but learning from failure helps you achieve even greater things.

CHRIS GORMAN, B. 1966

I learned that the only way you are going to get anywhere in life is to work hard at it. Whether you're a musician, a writer, an athlete, or a businessman, there is no getting around it. If you do, you'll win – If you don't, you won't.

BRUCE JENNER

No one ever pushes you toward freedom. You need to take that for yourself.

JOAN ERIKSON

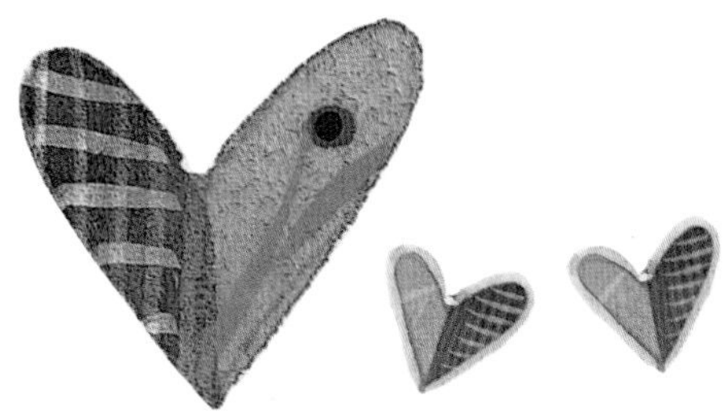

Don't let life discourage you;
everyone who got where he is
had to begin where he was.

RICHARD L. EVANS

Without a dream, without goals, we have no direction.

HOWARD BEHAR, B. 1944

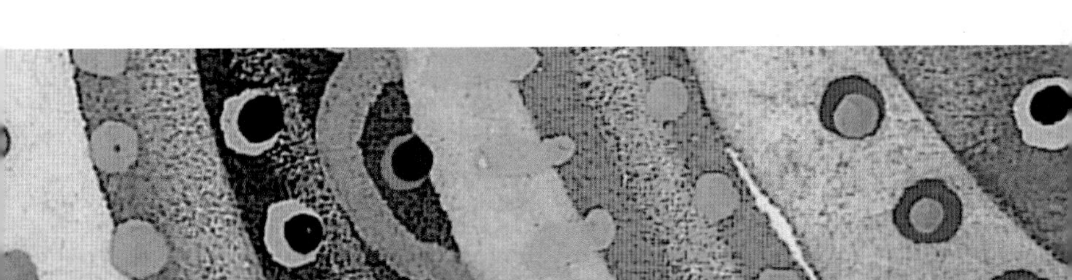

If you want to do something, do it.
Don't worry if it's right or wrong.
Don't worry whether it will work out or not.
And above all else don't worry
what other people think.

ROHANN CANDAPPA, B. 1962

Fear not that thy life shall
come to an end, but rather fear that
it shall never have a beginning.

JOHN HENRY 1801 – 1890

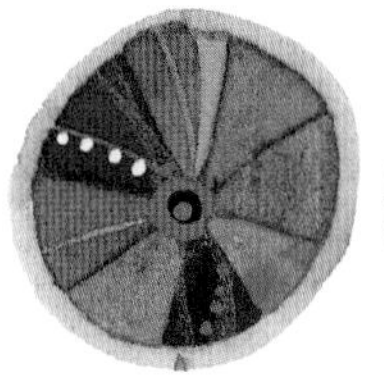
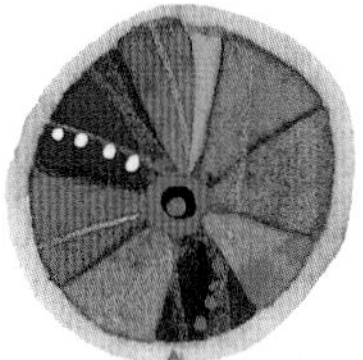
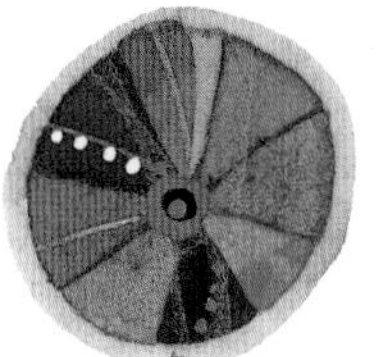
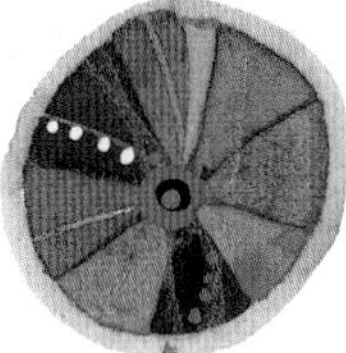

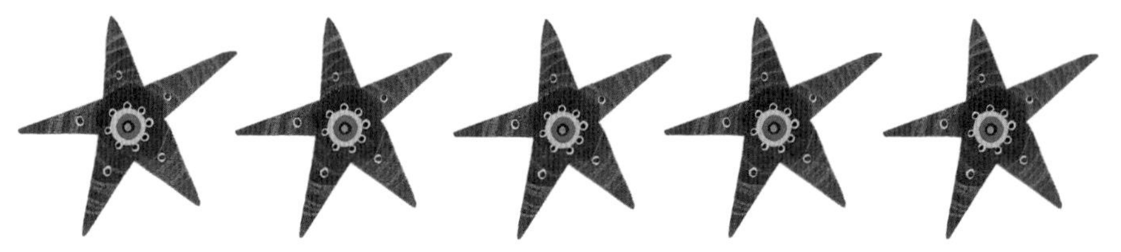

...don't let anyone
stand in the way of your goal.

DAME KELLY HOLMES, B. 1970

The beaten track does not lead to new pastures.

INDIRA GANDHI 1917 – 1984

You can have excellent music teachers, as you can art, maths and English teachers. You can have great sports coaches, but true genius, great artists, writers, musicians and gold medal winners tend to have the seed of genius inside them, they are winners inside long before they ever achieve greatness.

DR. DALTON EXLEY

We make little worlds of our lives
and place ourselves in the centre of them.
Understandably so, yet as dictators,
as kings and queens in our little kingdoms
why then are we so often miserable
and why do we hold ourselves back?
For what we have we really shouldn't
be able to stop smiling. Just being alive
is truly incredible if you ever stop
to really think about it.

DR. DALTON EXLEY

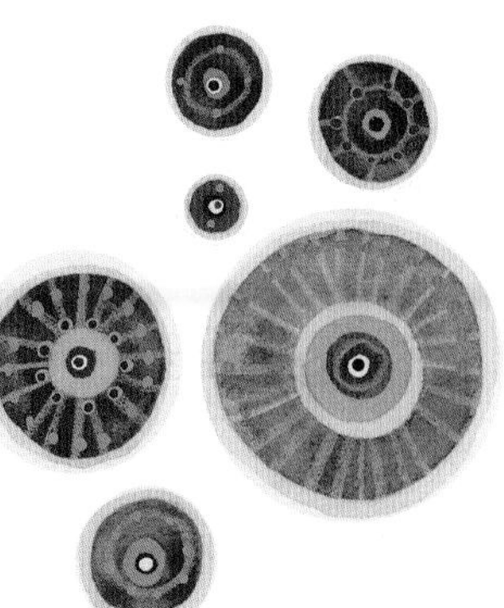

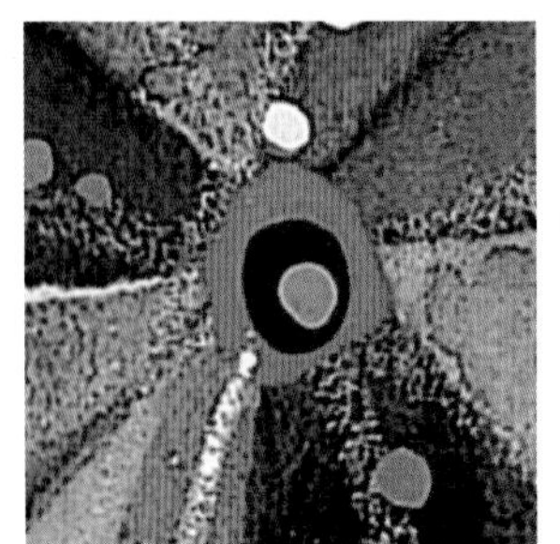
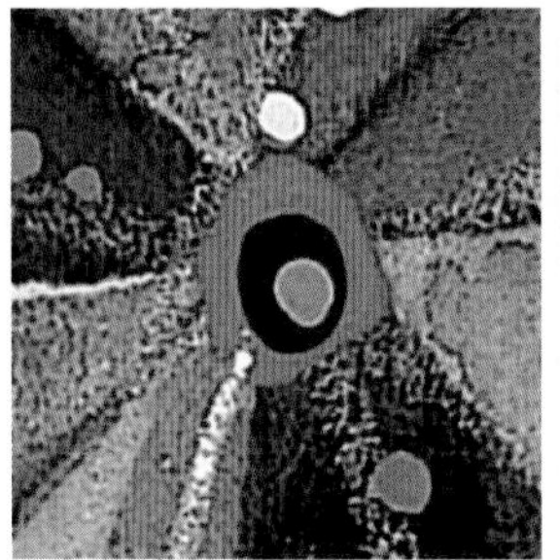
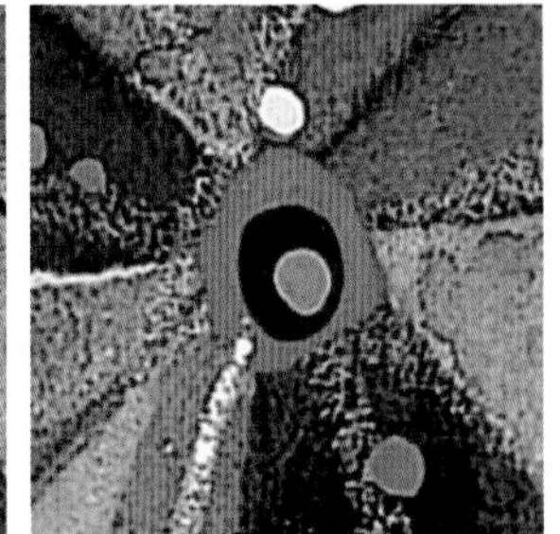

A PERSON IS NOT OLD UNTIL REGRETS TAKE THE PLACE OF DREAMS.

JOHN BARRYMORE 1882 – 1942

JULY 1

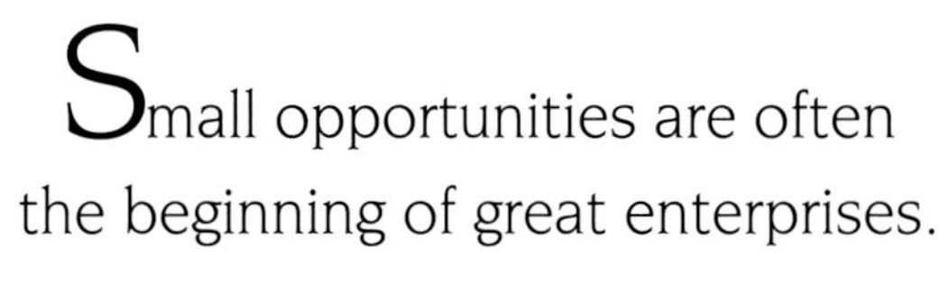

Small opportunities are often the beginning of great enterprises.

DEMOSTHENES 384 B.C – 322 B.C

Whatever you have, you ought to use; and whatever you do, you should do with all your might.

MARCUS TULLIUS CICERO 106 B.C. – 43 B.C

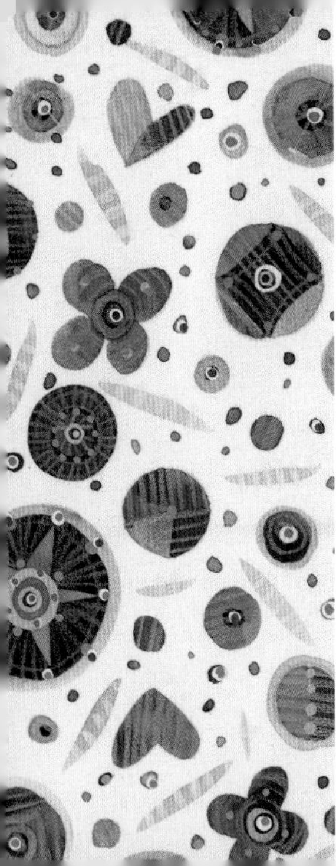

Don't let fear of failure, or lack of energy, or sheer laziness hold you back.

DAME KELLY HOLMES, B. 1970

As soon
as you feel too old
to do a thing,
do it.

MARGARET DELAND